# Liberating
# Limits

By the same author

*Growing Toward Wholeness*
*Becoming a Whole Family*

# Liberating Limits

## A Fresh Look At The Ten Commandments

### JOHN A. HUFFMAN, JR.

**WORD BOOKS**
PUBLISHER
WACO, TEXAS

ISBN 0-8499-2892-3
Library of Congress catalog card number: 79-63949
Printed in the United States of America

Unless otherwise noted, Scripture quotations are from the Revised
Standard Version of the Bible, copyright 1946, 1952, © 1971, 1973
by the Division of Christian Education of the National Council of the
Churches of Christ in the U.S.A., and used by permission. Quotation
from *The New English Bible*, © The Delegates of the Oxford University Press and The Syndics of The Cambridge University Press,
1961, 1970, is used by permission.

To my friends of the Key Biscayne Presbyterian Church, Key Biscayne, Florida; First Presbyterian Church of Pittsburgh, Pittsburgh, Pennsylvania; and St. Andrew's Presbyterian Church, Newport Beach, California—who have encouraged me in my study of the Scriptures and have helped me apply them to contemporary living

# CONTENTS

"You shall walk in all the way which the Lord your God has commanded you, that you may live, and that it may go well with you, and that you may live long in the land which you shall possess."

*Deuteronomy 5:33*

# 1.

# THE DON'TS THAT FREE

NO ONE needs to tell you that we are living in a time when our moral certainties are crumbling. I know you are concerned. I could bore you with statistics which document the increasing crime rate; lack of respect for law; the sexual revolution, with its increasing promiscuity, venereal disease, abortions, illegitimate births, and divorce; dishonesty in business and government; drug abuse; and alcoholism. Ours is an era marked by moral disintegration.

Even those of us who claim to be Christians are caught up in the same moral vagueness we lament in others but can end up coddling for ourselves. The vogue is freedom. Freedom to be ourselves. Freedom from the authority of others. And all too often, freedom from the authority of Almighty God. I've noticed that some of us who are most quick to point the condemning finger at the moral inequities in the lives of others, end up rationalizing our own shading of the truth in business, our own premarital or extramarital sexual involvements, our own cheating in the classroom, our own breaking of the law. Today's thrust is toward the positive. We want no negative.

9

We don't want anyone telling us what to do, what to say, and what to think. We chase bubbles of illusionary freedom, thinking that man has come of age. We turn our backs on what seem to be worn-out moral axioms that spoil our fun. For many of us, moral law—God's law—is out of date as we carve out our own way in a self-styled total freedom.

You and I owe ourselves a fresh look at the Ten Commandments. I'm convinced that there are certain don'ts that free. God has designated them for our well-being. Sir William Blackstone's serious reflections on jurisprudence concluded that "all civilized law begins with Moses, and rests solidly, four-square, on the rock of the Ten Commandments." Centuries ago, God revealed to his people on the move ten navigational aids. They need a good dusting off.

Before we look at them in more detail, let's examine two basic biblical presuppositions.

1. When you think you have liberated yourself from outdated divine law, you really are committing yourself to the ultimate in bondage.

I realize that moral law is coming under great question. Many argue that there is no such thing as propositional truth. One American philosopher has stated, "All is relative except the fact that all is relative. That is the only absolute." There are no eternal norms on which to build one's life. Existentialism marks the contemporary spirit. Smart people don't believe that there's a personal God who speaks in absolute terms.

I remember a classmate asking one of my ethics professors, "Is there any such thing as truth?" The professor answered, "No, not in an absolute way." We pressed him further, querying, "Then there's no definition for truth?" The professor scratched his head for a moment, then reassured us that he could define truth. He stated it in these terms: "Truth is truth for me." The implication was that every man must seek out that which is true for himself. Truth is relative. It is not absolute.

Philosophically, it would seem that this relativism leads to nihilism. Life is denied any long-range purpose. It loses its meaning. There's no creator and sustainer God who has revealed his moral law by which we must live. There's little room left for God to break into human history in the person of Jesus Christ offering redemption for our failure to honor that eternal law.

Not only is this philosophical relativism in secular academic circles making its profound impact on our society, we also find this questioning of divine law by some in the church who claim to be Christians. This "new morality" or "situational ethics" of men like John A. T. Robinson and Joseph Fletcher takes the position that moral absolutes are out of date. What we need today is a love ethic. It is irresponsible to make decisions based on some preconception of what is right and wrong. Instead one must examine all the dynamics surrounding the immediate situation in which one finds himself. This basic premise brings Joseph Fletcher, in his book *Situational Ethics*, to the deduction that any act—even lying, premarital sex, abortion, adultery, and murder—could be right, depending on the circumstances.

The tragic thing is that this thinking is being absorbed into the mainstream of so-called Christian theological and ethical thought. It is being articulated subtly from many American pulpits. It is being taught not so subtly in many of the classrooms of religion and ethics in our secular and denominational institutions. I'm not surprised when biblical sexual standards are ridiculed by non-Christian professors. However, I must admit that I was quite startled when I was laughed at by one of my seminary professors for articulating my commitment to biblical premarital chastity.

Those committed to the new morality think they've discovered freedom. There is an element of truth to what they're saying. Christ did state that the greatest commandment of all is, "You shall love the Lord your God with all your heart, and with all your soul, and with all your mind. This is the great and first commandment. And a second is like it, You shall love your neighbor as yourself" (Matt. 22:37–39). Ultimately the highest form of morality is based on love—God's love in Jesus Christ for us—and our response to his love in service for God and our fellowman. The unfortunate aspect is that it is difficult for us as sinful men and women to know how to apply love in every situation. We need guidance. We need some specific counsel that will help us. Otherwise love can be perverted as we rationalize ourselves into thinking that what we want to do at any given moment is right, blinding ourselves as to its negative implications for the future.

In February 1963, Harvard Divinity School hosted a conference of theologians and philosophers to discuss the new morality. *Time* magazine wrote a fascinating review. It outlined the presuppositions of situational ethics, noting that it was based on the ethic of love. *Time* lauded this idealism. Then at the end of the article, it made the tongue-in-cheek comment that pricked this idealistic balloon. It questioned what teenage couple involved in a passionate embrace in a parked car at two in the morning is capable in that situation of making a sober decision as to what is true love? What in the long run would be the best for each other?

Some normative guide is needed. Each of us in our passionate moments needs to know clearly what is right and what is wrong so that we will not lament in the years ahead an action which seemed so right at the time, but so wrong from hindsight.

Even the proponents of the new morality aren't as relativistic as they claim to be. Joseph Fletcher visited Yale University at the height of the Vietnam War. He called the war immoral. In the same lecture, he went on to develop his concept that there are no absolutes—just one great principle of love. A young Ph.D. candidate jumped to his feet during the discussion period and asked, "Dr. Fletcher, did I hear you say that the war in Southeast Asia is immoral?" "Yes," was the answer. This young professor then commented, "I take it then you have already defied your principle that there are no absolutes other than the principle of love." Fletcher was caught in his inconsistency. You cannot build an ethical system on that which is simply a positive. A positive itself will bring certain negatives. We can thank God that he has given some absolute guidelines. We are not dependent on our own consciences, which the Scriptures say can be perverted.

What I say comes as a result of having counseled with many persons who have come to me in tragic circumstances. They are products of this relativistic lifestyle. Many of these are young people who are indoctrinated in the new morality to the point that they had no normative moral values founded in divine edict. Therefore, they were left uncertain as to what was right and what was wrong. They thought they were liberated from the Ten Commandments. They thought that they were too mature to be boxed in by a bunch of petty rules until they awakened to find that their so-called freedom had turned to the bondage of separation from God, broken relationships with parents, lack of trust in a marriage partner, or an unplanned and unwanted pregnancy. Tears have streamed down their cheeks as broken lives have borne testimony to the bondage which comes through a false freedom—addiction to the idea that a man or a woman can get by on simply doing that which is right in his own eyes. Maude Royden of London City Temple fifty years ago stated it so bluntly, "You cannot

break the Ten Commandments; all you can do is break yourself against them!"

Is today's moral crisis really so different from that which has
gone before? I say, no! Every individual who has ever walked
the face of this earth has fought a moral battle. He or she has
had to make a decision as to whether to play the game of life
by God's rules or his or her own. It has sometimes been easier
than it is today to function by God's law. There have been societies that have structured their civil law upon God's revelation of himself and the propositional truths contained in
Scripture. Then there have been difficult times like those we
are facing today when societies have begun to reject this divine revelation and the individual battle becomes more difficult.

The breakdown we have today is a moral breakdown.
Technology is good. However, it increases the tendency of
making statistics out of persons. There is a losing of the self-
ness, a blending of individuals into a mass blur that comes
from our rejection of the moral absolutes revealed in God's
Word. It is impossible to maintain secular law where there is
the rejection of divine law. You can have statutes on the books,
but they become simply guides for a society to be broken at
will if one can get by with it. Break the law as long as you
don't get caught and have to pay the penalty. That's what
happened in those West Point cheating scandals of a few
years ago. Without confidence in the divinely revealed law, it
almost becomes moral to cheat. If everybody's doing it, you
have to do it to survive. Society creates its own standards, to
its own peril.

When you accept God's absolutes of right and wrong, you
know that you'll pay the results of breaking that law. It's not
a man-made standard. Even if you can get by with it, there
are certain moral consequences to an individual and to a society. Moral law is necessary for a society to function without

anarchy. It's necessary for an individual to function with a sense of fullness. Any individual who casts off obedience to God's moral law pays the price. The price is emptiness. Bishop Fulton Sheen has noted that there are "many lonely, empty lives which think they have been liberated from repressive morality but are wandering around looking for something to turn them on without obedience to divine law."

When you think you have liberated yourself from outdated divine law, you are really committing yourself to the ultimate in bondage.

2. Let's look at a second biblical principle. When you act in obedience to God's commandments, as restricting as they are to some of your animal instincts, you are truly set free. I'm the first to admit that you and I face tremendous pressures. We can philosophize about society. Whatever societal tendencies there are, are reflected in our own existence. I don't care how old you are or what your work may be, you and I face these same pressures toward moral relativism in business, home, and community. The person who thinks he is truly free may find that he is actually in bondage. The person who is willing to accept certain negatives as guidelines for his life, and who approaches them with the correct attitude, will find that he is actually free.

Let's look at this in a practical way. There are some don'ts which free. There are some negatives which produce positive results.

For example, take your child. Remember the first time that toddler headed for the open oven, mesmerized by the brilliant orange-red electrical coils? Did you sit back and pleasantly muse to yourself about the importance of your child making the right decision to meet the situation at hand? No, you swooped down on her grabbing her back from those redhot coils which could have maimed her for life. The stove became a "no-no." There was no room for experimentation. You knew what was best for your child. You made a law, a negative designed to set that child free from potential tragic burns.

Speed laws, when enforced, cut down on fatal accidents. I'll never forget this newspaper report. The headline read, "Man Ticketed, Then He Dies." This report followed:

> Twenty miles up the road after he was ticked for speeding, a Polk County man was killed Saturday in a crash at a speed estimated by the Highway Patrol at better than 100 miles an hour.
>
> Clarence Hall, 36, of Auburndale, was stopped and given a citation in Marion County on Interstate 75 south of Gainesville.
>
> He lost control of his car 10 miles northwest of here and crashed into an overpass guard rail. The car jumped the rail, became airborne, and sailed 112 feet before landing on its top.

This fellow thought he was free. Free to drive the way he wanted to. He was. He did. He was in bondage. He killed himself in the process of being free. He ignored the restraints of society and paid the price.

Pain restrains us from doing what we know will hurt or kill us. I hate pain. I'd love to live free from pain. But thank God for pain. It's a negative that becomes a positive in alerting us to the fact that something's wrong in a physical way.

I may think that I'm free and take an elevator to the top of the tallest building in town. If I could find an open perch, I could stand out looking down at the plaza below. I'm free to jump, perfectly free. Fortunately, there's a law that I sense within me and that I've observed on the part of others: if I take that leap, it's very doubtful that I'll be able to fly. You've dreamed of flying, haven't you? Flying is one of my greatest dreams. Yet I'm realistic enough to know that in the real life, I can't do it simply by flapping my arms. I'm free to try.

Thank God that some persons have the discipline to say no

to play and yes to difficult study and practice. This gives the skill to the surgeon whose delicate expertise will remove that tumor from the brain. It was good to know when, several years ago, our doctor prepared to remove my wife's kidney, that he hadn't been up drinking all night. He was free to do whatever he wanted, but the discipline to say no produced an even greater freedom marked by professional precision.

God's law as revealed in the Ten Commandments and throughout the rest of Scripture at times gets negative. Never is it negative for any other purpose than to bring us into ultimate freedom. Read the events surrounding God's revelation to Moses. God didn't just list the Ten Commandments in a negative way. He gave his list of "don'ts," but he went on to articulate positive results. He gave promises that are available to those who obey his law. He listed consequences that are constructive and positive, pointing out the healthy results that come from a strict adherence to some of the don'ts of a God-ordained nature. He says: "Oh that they had such a mind as this always, to fear me and to keep all my commandments, that it might go well with them and with their children for ever!" (Deut. 5:29).

This is the yearning heart of God. He wants us to respect him in a way that leads us to keep his commandments. It's not to spoil our fun. It's for the purpose that it might be well with us and with our children forever.

Moses picks up on this theme. He restates to the people of Israel God's charge combined with God's promises: "You shall be careful to do therefore as the Lord your God has commanded you; you shall not turn aside to the right hand or to the left. You shall walk in all the way which the Lord your God has commanded you, that you may live and that it may go well with you, and that you may live long in the land which you shall possess" (Deut. 5:32–33).

Just as there are don'ts which free in the physical area, there are similar spiritual laws. When God tells us not to work on the seventh day, he means it. He means it for our good. He's trying to protect us from ourselves. He knows how we function best. We can't survive seven days of work week in and week out.

When he says, "Thou shalt not commit adultery," and enumerates the other sexual prohibitions, he is freeing us by his restrictions. I talked with a fellow who told me that he had made all the prostitutes from Paris to Athens—and all the time he was scared to death of catching VD. Freedom. . . . You call that freedom? He had his kicks. I have yet to run into anybody who's caught venereal disease when both the husband and wife are faithful to each other.

"You shall not bear false witness against your neighbor." Some very prominent public officials would have been spared humiliation and jail terms if they had simply told the truth—instead of lying.

"Neither shall you steal." How many persons are behind bars today, locked up, deprived of their freedom because they exercised their liberty to steal? How many others are locked in behind the bars labeled "guilty conscience" for their failure to play the game by God's ground rules? Oh, it would be nice to be able to pick up that ten-speed bike and not have to work for weeks and weeks to get it. But the same thing that goes for the other guy goes for you. The same thing that goes for you goes for the other guy, because he can pick up your ten-speed bike without working weeks and weeks for it.

These are just some of the reasons for moral law. Biblical scholars continue to debate the primary uses of God's law. I believe that the Ten Commandments and the other biblical instructions serve three functions.

1. God's law polices secular society. Have you ever thought of that? Even if we reject Jesus Christ, moral law, the law of

God, the very presence of that law, enhances life's quality. If enough people in a society accept God's Word as absolute, that society can function with a stability otherwise unavailable. As respect for God's law erodes, social stability breaks down. God's law serves as a policeman.

2. The second use of the law is to confront us with the fact that we are sinners. Look over the Ten Commandments. Can you claim perfection? If so, you deserve a citation. It's only against such a high moral standard that you and I are confronted with our sin. God is a righteous God. His standards are high. The starting point in becoming a Christian is the acknowledgment that we are sinners. Once we confess that we are lawbreakers who need forgiveness, then we can experience God's grace.

3. A third use of the law is for the believer who comes to faith. For this person the law is a "schoolmaster," an instructor that shows us how to live our lives in the most creative way possible.

If we're willing to obey God's law, we qualify for his promises, ". . . that ye may live. . . ." God's interested in us. He wants us to enjoy life. He wants us to live it to the fullest. If you're a young person, you may think that all these negatives prescribed by your God and enforced by your parents are robbing you of having a good time. Instead they're protecting you, and me, from our self-destructive bent, our own masochistic tendency to destroy ourselves.

Then he promises that if we keep these commandments ". . . it may go well with you. . . ." That's what Paul was talking about when he shared with his friends at Philippi that God would supply all their needs according to his riches and glory by Christ Jesus. It doesn't say that we'll have everything. He does promise provision. If you'll forgive my coining a word, he offers us "wellness," which simply means that we may prosper in those things essential to our ultimate well-being. It doesn't promise a forty thousand dollar a year job, two cars, prestige in the community. It promises to meet our needs.

Then he promises "that you may live long in the land which you shall possess." For some this actually means a quantitative life extension. The person who disobeys God's commandments dissipates his or her physical and emotional resources to the point that it sometimes shortens the actual lifespan. For some of us, this is a qualitative promise. True discipleship may even shorten our lifespan, but in the process we will have an increase in quality, knowing that our lives are expendable for our Lord. Thirty obedient years are longer in richness than ninety years marked by self-indulgence.

Granted, God's standard is high. However, adherence to his ground rules makes life all the more fun. We can create our own rules, make them less demanding, lower them to a comfortable standard. In the process we've pulled out from under ourselves the potential for true happiness. Take too many "mulligans" in golf or accept too many "gimmee" putts and you'll score better. But this raises some questions. Where does par come in? Who speaks for par? Who sets the standards that make life worth living? By whose rules would you rather live? Your own, which lessen life's quality? Or by God's, whose don'ts truly free?

"I am the Lord your God, who brought you out of the land of Egypt, out of the house of bondage. You shall have no other gods before me."
*Exodus 20:2–3*

# 2.

# NO OTHER GODS

TWENTY-TWO years ago, through a unique set of circumstances, it was my privilege to spend the better part of the day in Hollywood, California, with Cecil B. DeMille. You can imagine my thrill as a high school senior to have one of the all-time great movie producers take me under his wing.

At the time, my father was president of a summer theological seminary. Fund-raising was one of his major responsibilities. Biblical studies was a major part of the curriculum. Father had heard of Cecil DeMille's interest in biblical archaeology. Perhaps he could interest him in giving some financial support. So while our family was spending a Christmas vacation in southern California, my father endeavored to make an appointment. At first he received the typical runaround. Finally, Mr. DeMille's secretary, somewhat fascinated as to why a Protestant minister from the Midwest would want to talk with a Hollywood movie mogul, set up the appointment. There was only one hitch. It would not be at the studio. It would be a brief meeting at his home in the Hollywood hills.

Dad took me along. I'll never forget driving up to that majestic hillside mansion and being escorted alongside my father through opulently furnished rooms into the presence of Mr. DeMille. I can't remember what the two men said to each other. I also don't know whether or not he ever made a contribution. What I do remember is the gracious way he treated me. He showed the two of us around his home. Just as we were parting, he said, "By the way, son, I have some things I need to do this morning, but later on I'm going down to the Paramount Studios. Have you ever been on a movie set? Why don't you and your sister join me for lunch?"

We were there all right. Eighteen-year-old John with his fourteen-year-old kid sister, Miriam. Mom and Dad weren't invited, which made it all the more special. They dropped us off at the entrance to the studios. We were cleared through security. The secretary led us to Mr. DeMille's office. Then he personally escorted us around the set. He introduced us to Charlton Heston, Claire Bloom, and Yul Brynner, who were taking a break on the set of *The Buccaneer*. We watched the affable Jerry Lewis do several takes in *Rock-a-Bye Baby*. Then we walked into the commissary for lunch. There, dazzle-eyed as we were surrounded by the stars, we sat down at the table. The waiter brought our menus.

One aspect of that day will never be forgotten. There on the front of the menu were these words, embossed in large print: "CECIL B. DeMILLE SAYS, 'DON'T JUST ACT THE TEN COMMANDMENTS. LIVE THEM!'" Underneath were listed all Ten Commandments, directly out of the Old Testament.

In his own way, this man had observed the same thing that perceptive persons have observed through all human history, that there was some persuasive moral quality about these standards. They were more than good box office. They were worth living, no matter how difficult that practice might be.

You and I live in a world that quickly becomes a jungle if

there are no arbitrary moral restraints. Only moral power can defend against the abuses of an atomic age. Society must be brought into conformity with this moral order or it will destroy itself. The best articulation of it is found in the Ten Commandments as interpreted by Jesus Christ. Perhaps we could paraphrase Mr. DeMille's admonition: "Don't just believe the Ten Commandments, live them!" Whenever ethical systems are subjected to human scrutiny, the Ten Commandments surface as the greatest basis for societal and personal conduct. Alexander Maclaren wrote:

> An obscure tribe of Egyptian slaves plunges into the desert to hide from pursuit, and emerges, after forty years, with a code gathered into "ten words," so brief, so complete, so intertwining morality and religion, so free from local or national pecularities, so close fitting to fundamental duties, that it is today, after more than three thousand years, authoritative in the most enlightened peoples. The voice that spoke from Sinai reverberates in all lands. The Old World had other lawgivers who professed to formulate their precepts by divine inspiration: they are all fallen silent. But this voice, like the trumpet on that day, waxes louder and louder as the years roll. Whose voice was it? The only answer explaining the supreme purity of the commandments, and their immortal freshness, is found in the first sentence of this paragraph, "God spake all these words." [1]

As I struggle to live life with a sense of purpose, I'm increasingly overwhelmed with the fact that God spoke. Not only that; God continues to speak. God speaks in an authoritative fashion through his Ten Commandments. The first four outline our religious duties. The final six state our moral responsibilities. Commandments 1 through 4 show us how to function in relationship to our God. Commandments 5 through 10 get specific about the negative impact of wrong deeds, wrong words, and wrong thoughts. They are specifically recorded in Exodus, chapter 20. They are restated by Moses in Deuteronomy, chapter 5. He takes that occasion to amplify and even change the wording so that a new generation will receive a slightly better understanding of God's authoritative will. He calls Israel together and says to them: "Hear, O Israel, the statutes and the ordinances which I speak in your hearing this day, and you shall learn them and be careful to do them" (Deut. 5: 1). This is a specific call to obedience.

As we look at the First Commandment, there are two specific words which God wants us to hear.

The first word God speaks is "I am the Lord your God. . . ." In this day of relativistic ethics when moral certainties are being questioned, in this day of the new morality and situation ethics, it is essential that you and I hear the voice of God. It's important that we find his direction.

It's fascinating to note that when God delivered his Commandments, he took time to preface his remarks with a statement that provides the basis for our obedience. He didn't just authoritatively say, "Here are ten things you shall not do." Instead, in a simple direct way he reminded the people that he was a living God, personally concerned for each of them. His initial remark is not a command. Instead, it is the basis on which all the commands rest. He reminds his people that he is the God who had brought them out of the land of Egypt, out of the house of bondage. The starting point for obedience is an awareness of God's fatherhood, an awareness of our sonship, an awareness of our family relationship to him.

It's one thing while lunching in the Paramount commissary casually to peruse as some ancient moral creed the Ten Commandments printed on the menu. It's another to hear their Author confront us in intimate personal terms with the words "I am the Lord your God."

The word "your" appears in the singular. It applies to the people of Israel; it also addresses individual persons. There are many who read the Ten Commandments, sense their moral power, but don't obey them because their Author is not "their" God. These words are binding only upon those who are true believers—who have a personal relationship with the one who claims to be our God.

When we were growing up, as youngsters we never felt we had to obey someone else's parents, unless our parents had specifically told us that for a certain amount of time we were to take orders from another. Never does a babysitter have the ultimate authority of a father and a mother. Parenthood has deeply imbedded in it a nature of loving concern. This, in turn, demands obedience.

To obey the Ten Commandments without having a personal relationship with God ties us up in legalistic knots. It's like trying to obey a law without having enough strength to obey that law. It is only as we are genuinely exposed to what God is endeavoring to accomplish in our life, that obedience to his eternal law takes on the dimension of exciting creativity instead of stale oppressive discipline. A basic biblical message is that God has created us, and he continues to sustain us, even as he sees our own bent toward rebellion and our own tendency to complicate our lives with that which hurts and distracts from his very best. He gave himself to us as our Savior. The children of Israel saw this in the context of their deliverance out of Egypt. We benefit from the New Testament. We see this in the context of God's becoming a man in Jesus Christ and providing atonement for our sins. It's only after we come to an awareness of all that he has done for us—being set free by our faith, our trust, our confidence in him—that God leads us into the new, exciting dimensions of what is available if we live our lives in obedience to his commandments. Only divine grace can enable us to keep his commands. It's that grace which enables us to not only hear his words "I am the Lord your God," but to respond with the words "my Lord and my God."

God's second word builds on this positive affirmation. It's the first of ten don'ts which free. God says, "You shall have no other Gods before me."

It's difficult for you and me fully to appreciate the circumstances facing the people of Israel at the time God presented the law to Moses. Polytheism was rampant. This gargantuan monotheistic statement was revolutionary in its impact. The Middle East had never heard these words so clearly stated. There were gods and goddesses for everything. There was a god of the sun, a god of the rain, a goddess of fertility. There were the gods of war, the gods of peace, the individual god for each family. There were as many gods as there were countries. Isis was supreme in Egypt. Moloch and Baal ruled over Canaan. Everytime the wandering peoples crossed the border they came under the jurisdiction of another god. Now they are told that only one God matters. No others count. It doesn't make any difference how far you travel or whose country you're in, this God goes with you. No other god is to be worshiped. Wander after other gods and you'll end up in trouble. Some would do it and find out the hard way. So God is saying, "Don't go native."

Centuries later, Elijah remembered those words when he and a few of his faithful contemporaries would not bend their knee to Baal even though King Ahab and Queen Jezebel had done so. Not even the king of Israel could make Baal god. Nor could the conquering king Nebuchadnezzar many years later claim ultimate allegiance from Shadrach, Meshach, and Abednego. They would rather be thrown into a fiery furnace than deny their Lord. Daniel would rather be thrown to hungry

lions than compromise his spiritual integrity. Their times were so different from today's. Or—were they?

Who is this God who demands such allegiance? He is identified in the preamble. He's Jehovah who says, "I am that I am." He is the eternal self-existent One. Or, putting it another way, he is the One who says, "I will be that I will be," which simply means that he will prove himself in our own experience. This was his word to Moses in his encounter with the burning bush. This God is identified as Elohim. He is the Almighty God who had proven his mercy in the deliverance from servitude in Egypt and would continue to reveal himself as his people entered the Promised Land. He was the One who had made a covenant with Adam and Eve that one would come who would bruise the head of the serpent. He had renewed this covenant in a specific way with Abraham. He rearticulated it at Sinai. He put his precise signature on it when he became a man in the person of Jesus Christ. Jesus talked about this Almighty God, teaching his disciples to pray, "Our Father." He was the father of all men, not just Jews. Then Jesus adds those startling statements, "He who has seen me has seen the Father . . ." (John 14:9). "I and the Father are one" (John 10:30).

Who, or what, is your God? How do you stand on this issue? This question is not just for non-Christians; I address this to you even if you are a Christian. Respond authentically, within yourself: Who is your god? Or what are your gods?

There are many definitions for god. Paul Tillich called God the "ground of all being"—the very basis of our existence. Karl Barth called God the Wholly Other, the transcendent one, the one above us, beyond us, who is capable of breaking into our lives. Martin Luther noted that a person's god is to be found in that to which he gives his final obedience, and from which he expects his highest help. In a polytheistic world, only one god demands ultimate supreme allegiance. Allegiance is not to be shared with any other god.

Therefore, I think in a practical way we must make a distinction between *God* with a capital *G*, and *god* with a small *g*. God with a capital *G* is that One who created and sustains us, whereas, the god or gods with a small *g* are those that have supreme authority in our lives, those to which we have made our ultimate commitment in life. They need not be the true God.

Who, then, is your god? Your immediate response may be, "Well, of course, Jesus Christ is my God." Is he really? Does he have your full allegiance? Or are there other gods which tend to crowd him out? Do you think that you are worshiping Jesus Christ, only to find in reality that you are worshiping a different set of gods, deceiving yourself all the while? Any god who does not command your total allegiance cannot really be God.

Perhaps your business is your god. Your ultimate commitment is to your profit and loss statement. There is time for Jesus Christ on Sunday morning, but really none the rest of the week. Your profession is enormously important. Your main effort goes into doing a successful job.

I would be totally dishonest if I pretended that I did not have a similar struggle. My work is very important to me. I believe I have a call of God into the ministry. This does not rule out a tendency for my career, as good as it is, to become god—getting in the way of the Lord God, Jehovah, who has revealed himself in the person of Jesus Christ. I yearn to be a success. I yearn to preach sermons that are scintillating. I want people to like me and genuinely benefit from my labors. Nowhere in the Scriptures does it say we are not to be a success in our vocation. However, it does say, "You shall have no other gods before me." When our work draws top priority,

we can be sure we are not living in obedience to God.

Perhaps your social set is your god. If so, your life is being shaped by your friends. One teenage girl was perceptive enough to say, "People stick in crowds. Kids like me love to have our crowd. Mostly the crowd becomes god." Is your crowd your god? Not just teenagers are at fault—how we adults blind ourselves to our own compulsions in this quest! We too want to be part of the "in group"—in dress, actions, thought patterns, and beliefs.

Possibly the best way to find out what your god really is is to check out your daydreams. What do you muse about in your most introspective moments? What are your casual thoughts when the sermon gets a bit dull and your mind wanders off? Answer these questions and you'll get a pretty good idea. Perhaps pleasure is your god—golf, fishing, hunting, or tennis; food and beverage; sex, in fantasy or in reality. All of these are good, but not good enough to be your God.

Another way to check out who your gods are is to take a look at your checkbook and see where your money is going. You know and I know that we don't spend our money on things that are unimportant to us. The proportions of your money that go for pleasure, family, God, come as an insightful revelation of your true priorities.

Some make a god out of country, giving their primary allegiance to their nation. Thank God for America, but don't let America become your God.

All of these things are so good. How easy it is to get caught up with our everyday concerns, allowing them to become gods.

Remember the parable about the marriage feast? Jesus told about a king who gave a marriage feast for his son. He sent his servants to call all those who were invited to the marriage feast. They wouldn't come. Again he sent other servants to alert the guests that the feast was ready. The guests made light of it.

One went off to his farm, another to his business, while the rest mistreated the servants. Then the king, upset that the original guests didn't respond, opened up the invitation to anyone who would respond. You know what Jesus was talking about. The servants were the prophets, John the Baptist, and himself. Those who turned down the invitation were the Jews.

However, there's another message contained in this parable. The persons who ignored the invitation were simply busy with good things. There's nothing wrong with farming or business or family life unless these lesser priorities become god and stand between us and the Lord our God who has brought us out of sin's bondage. You and I can fret about life, health, finances, and children to the point that we discredit our God by enthroning these lesser concerns in his place.

I'm convinced that everyone has a god. Skeptical? I'll wager you still have one. One day the church phone rang. One of the secretaries picked it up. The young male voice at the other end asked, "Is this the Presbyterian Church?" "Yes," she replied. "Well, I'm an atheist! I don't need you!" Bang went the receiver. I'll never forget hearing Anthony Newley sing a song on the *Tonight Show.* I had never heard it before. Anne and I were both half asleep and half watching the show when the words started to hit me like a sledge hammer. I jumped out of bed, went over to the dresser, grabbed my notebook and pen to jot them down. It went something like this: "I need no God. . . . As long as I have me, I'm all I need. . . . If I have me, who needs people? . . . The guy you see at the top of the heap will be me."

The man who thinks he doesn't need God has a god. He is his own god. God says, "You shall have no other gods before me."

Let's be honest with ourselves. So many gods compete for our attention. God says, "You must have me. What good would it

be if you had the whole world but didn't have me? It would rattle around in you like a solitary walnut in an otherwise empty canister."

The Apostle Paul stated in these exhilarating words,

> Have this mind among yourselves, which is yours in Christ Jesus, who, though he was in the form of God did not count equality with God a thing to be grasped, but emptied himself, taking the form of a servant, being born in the likeness of men. And being found in human form he humbled himself and became obedient unto death, even death on a cross. Therefore God has highly exalted him and bestowed on him the name which is above every name, that at the name of Jesus every knee should bow, in heaven and on earth and under the earth, and every tongue confess that Jesus Christ is Lord, to the glory of God the Father (Phil. 2: 5–11).

Who, or what, is your god? Is he powerful or powerless? Is it capable of satisfying your deepest needs or is it draining you emotionally and personally? Come to the risen Christ. Come with all your problems, doubts, and questions. Confess him as God. Worship him and find his resources for creative existence.

The last sermon of Dwight L. Moody was on "Excuses." He narrated the parable of the marriage feast and closed with the characteristic appeal:

> Suppose we should write out tonight this excuse, how would it sound? "To the King of Heaven: While sitting in Convention Hall, Kansas City, Mo., November 16, 1899, I received a very pressing invitation from one of your servants to be present at the marriage supper of your only begotten Son. I pray Thee have me excused." Would you sign that? . . . Just let me write out another answer. "To the King of Heaven: While sitting in Convention Hall, Kansas City, Mo., November 16, 1899, I received a pressing

invitation from one of your messengers to be present at the marriage supper of your only begotten son. I hasten to reply: By the grace of God I will be present."

With these words upon his lips, America's great evangelist ended his career. And a worthy end it was, for one of these responses or the other each of us must give. Are we too busy to let God be God?

"You shall not make for yourself a graven image, or any likeness of anything that is in heaven above, or that is in the earth beneath, ·or that is in the water under the earth; you shall not bow down to them or serve them; for I the Lord your God am a jealous God. . . ."

*Exodus 20:4–5*

# 3.

# HAVE THINGS TAKEN OVER?

W HEREAS the First Commandment states, "You shall have no other Gods before me," this Second Commandment stresses that nothing is to get between us and the One True God. Whereas the First Commandment emphasizes the unity which is his, nothing should vie with him for our ultimate commitment. This commandment helps us strip away those things which could ultimately compete with him. The first states that there's one true object of worship. The second tells us the right way to worship. The first calls us to worship God alone. The second calls for purity and spirituality in our approach to him.

As closely related as these two seem, I trust you will catch the difference. It is impossible to keep the Second Commandment of allowing no idols if we have broken the First Commandment of worshiping no other gods. More subtly, the breaking of the Second Commandment—allowing other things, as good as they are, to get between God and ourselves—inevitably leads to the breaking of the First Commandment. For these other things tend to become gods.

As complex as this may seem, it's actually quite simple. The First Commandment describes our ultimate destination. The Second Commandment sketches a roadmap. Fortunately, we have a guide. We're not alone in our endeavor to worship the One True God who became a man in Jesus Christ. As we humbly admit our failures, the risen Christ sets us free from guilt to productive living. Our worship is enabled by the Holy Spirit. Biblical instructions provide help to get us where we're going.

Imagine that you are planning a trip from Pittsburgh to Los Angeles. You'd eventually get there by heading southwest, stopping at filling stations for directions. You'd make innumerable detours on roads that were going the right direction but were not the quickest route. The God who loves us has given us a roadmap. The Bible is his Word. It sets down commandments, propositional truths that can steer us, helping us to arrive more quickly at our ultimate destination of glorifying God and enjoying him forever. Follow it closely. You'll avoid endless detours. Your path will be straight, your direction precise.

The Apostle Paul muses about a self-destructing human tendency. He says that written into both God's natural revelation through his creation and his special revelation through his Word is truth about himself. In the first chapter of Romans, he describes our basic human tendency to exchange truth about God for a lie. We think we are wise. We have a glimpse of the One True God. In our self-styled wisdom, we become fools as we exchange "the glory of the immortal God for images resembling mortal man or birds or reptiles" (Rom. 1:23).

Paul goes on to state that many persons have exchanged "the truth about God for a lie and worshiped and served the creature rather than the Creator, who is blessed for ever!"

The Second Commandment states this basic principle: Our spiritual worship of the Triune God can quickly turn to idolatry. Instead of worshiping the Creator, our very worship effort can become creature-centered.

What, then, is idolatry? Our minds flash quickly to the pagan religions with their divine archives. Each god is represented by some visible image created by human hands. God is reduced to a material object having human or animal characteristics. Perhaps you've walked through the marketplaces of Asia or Africa and seen gods for sale. I've stood before idol shrines in Kamakura, Nara, Taipei, Bangkok, Singapore, Calcutta, and New Delhi, watching men, women, and children fall prostrate before idols. They were focusing their worship on a human creation, a great Buddha which stands as a tangible substitute for a distant god.

Does this mean that we're not allowed to use any physical objects in our worship? Some have applied these words quite literally. The Puritans allowed no paintings or sculptures in their worship sanctuaries. Some even opposed organs. The Eastern Orthodox, interpreting these words literally, allow only icons, flat pictures of Jesus, the Virgin Mary, and the saints. No multidimensional sculpture or images are allowed. Roman and Anglo-Catholics, along with the Lutherans, see this command modified by the Incarnation. No images are allowed representing God the Father, but statues of Jesus and the saints are used as worship aids.

The Bible is quite clear that we are not to reduce God to some man-made image and then focus our worship on that image. However, God's Word does not denounce religious objects per se. The same God who disallowed the worship of images commanded that his people build the Temple at Jerusalem. He gave elaborate specifications for that temple, warning that any material symbol in worship has its dangers. One danger is that we will lift up the symbol to his level. The other is that we will drag God down to the level of the symbol. Instead, he calls us to spiritual worship. We are to worship him, not things. An image can become an emotive expression about God that reshapes him to our own specifications. What was once alive can quickly die out. What was pulsating can quickly calcify. What was spiritual can become carnal. What was a vehicle to spirituality can become the end of spirituality.

There's a much more subtle idolatry that does not reside alone in the creation of images, but also in symbols. The cross of Jesus Christ stands out as the key symbol. The bread and the wine are tokens which trigger our memories. The dove represents the Holy Spirit which hovers over God's people. Use these symbols. Don't let them use you!

The idolatry that comes closest to gripping modern Christians is the making of images and symbols to satisfy the craving of our hearts for sensuous worship. What I mean is that any worship that keeps our soul among things, no matter how good those things may be, is idolatry. Instead, our worship should lift us up beyond the world of tangible objects to a spiritual oneness with God Almighty. The opposite of idolatry is spiritual worship. This worship is intellectually and morally elevating. It is the experience of a soul moving Godward, beyond itself and all the things which keep it earthbound. The best images and aids to worship, as good as they may be, can become tangible blocks which hold us to this world. Yes, you and I, God's creatures, can end up worshiping what God has created instead of the Creator.

This sounds pretty complicated, doesn't it? Your immediate reaction may be, "What in the world are you talking about? I don't have any idols!"

Are you certain? It's easy for some very good things which once were spiritual channels to become idols. A vehicle which helped carry us to God can become an obstacle, tripping us into idolatry, subtly seducing us into disobeying the Second Commandment. Satan will try to get us to worship anything, however good. All he wants to do is distract us from God himself. He will even elevate the Bible, the crucifix, a doctrinal system, the cross, the church, in a way which distracts us from the Lord. These worthy objects can stand between us and the Lord and ultimately become gods themselves, leading us into a disobedience of his First Commandment not to have any other gods before him.

I like to have my life neatly packaged. For some reason, God didn't choose neatly to package the Christian faith. I yearn for a theological system that itemizes everything about God in a logical order. I believe the Bible is the only infallible rule of faith and practice. Something in me wants to worship the Bible. You see, I have a hard time handling the intangible and God is intangible. Give me an object that will help me touch him and when I still can't touch all of him but can touch all of that object, I'm inclined to embrace it instead of him.

I guess, in short, I feel a lot more comfortable with the god I've created. One about whom I know everything. One who doesn't challenge me. One whose word I can edit to my own wishes. One who affirms what I already believe. One who doesn't make me feel uncomfortable with the inconsistencies in my life. I want a god who likes what I like and hates what I hate, a god who wants my advice. So while Moses is up on the mountain confronting his pure, unadulterated truth, I'm down in the valley shaping my golden calf, polishing my object of worship to the One True God who so quickly becomes embodied in the golden calf. It's like making a fetish of your lover's picture. You're so mesmerized by her image imprinted on paper that you don't sense her real presence entering the room. It's taking that brazen serpent that was lifted up in the wilderness through which God's healing power flowed and institutionalizing it in the Temple so that hundreds of years later, it had to be smashed by Hezekiah's reform.

I realize this is pretty complicated conversation. Let's move from the general theological realm to the specifics, listing some of our modern-day idols.

A method of worship can become an idol. You may have been raised within a high church liturgy; you may have used a prayerbook with its set pattern. A Gothic cathedral with its stained glass windows expands you spiritually, lifting you up toward God. You find it impossible to sense God's presence unless you're in that environment. You become nervous with a more informal spiritual expression. The free flow of emotion turns you off. On the other hand, your background may be one of spontaneous worship. You like the informality. For you the written prayer is cold, sterile, spiritually lifeless. The wearing of vestments, the lighting of candles, the singing of Gregorian chants turns you off. You even have a tough time with Bach. You yearn for the simple, relaxed setting of the small family church. You prefer gospel choruses.

Either of these methods, with their many variations, can be spiritually powerful, giving you direct access to God. At the same time, any particular worship style which once transported you into God's presence can become rigid, an idol that stands between you and your Lord. You become bound to the method, not to the living Christ.

Far from being bothered by denominational differences, I thank God for denominations. The Pentecostal, the Baptist, the Presbyterian, the Episcopalian, the Roman Catholic do not all respond with the same outward expression. Yet when each of these faiths is taken seriously, the inward result is the same. Picture two deaf men sitting on a railroad track, unaware a train is barreling down the track toward them. Just a split second before their lives would have been snuffed out, a bystander rushes to their aid, pulling them from the track and saving their lives. One of the men sits down, bows his head in quiet awe contemplating his deliverance. The other man starts jumping around. With a hilarity, a joyous verbal outburst, he emotionally elaborates on his deliverance. Both have received the same deliverance. (The first man is probably a Presbyterian; the second, a Pentecostal!) One dare not judge the other for at that point he narrows and makes rigid his emotive approach until it becomes an idol. His denominational affiliation and the temperamental expression it reveals can block out our awareness of how great God is. Or another way of putting it, God is not a Baptist.

Individual leaders can become our idols. You may have a preacher or a teacher who has meant a lot to you. But the day comes when that person moves on, and you can no longer have that closeness in which you grew so quickly in your Christian life. Your faith becomes stalemated. Your understanding of the Scriptures stands pat. That person was so important to you. When you think of your faith, you think of that person and those past dynamic days.

Some time ago I was the guest speaker at a women's retreat. One woman confided, "My husband and I were deeply touched by a pastor we had many years ago. Our lives were changed through the impact of his ministry. Then we moved to this city. For several years we were restless. We couldn't find a church home. We couldn't find another minister who pleased us. You know, suddenly we awakened to the fact that we had made an idol out of our previous pastor. We had allowed the way God had worked in our lives through him to become rigid to the point that we were unwilling to let God work in a fresh new way through another minister who was gifted along different lines. Our spiritual growth was stunted by years as a result of our attachment to an individual man."

Other people can become idols. Spiritual hero worship—

even if that spiritual hero is Billy Graham—is idolatry. Truth comes only from God. He chooses to transmit it through human beings who are empowered by his Holy Spirit. When that transmitter—as great as he may be as a teacher, preacher, friend—becomes the source of truth for us, we have an idol. That image needs to be smashed before we can again have vital contact with the Living God.

Another potential idol is our theological creed. The Apostles' Creed, the Westminster Confession, and the other great historic confessions are our human endeavors to systematize faith's cognitive content so that it can be passed on from one generation to another. Creeds are necessary, protecting us against heresy which can erode historic Christianity. At the same time, creeds can get between us and God. But God is bigger than our confession. Never forget that creeds are man-made, shaped by human hands and minds. Never allow a creed to become your idol!

Spiritual experience which once was vital can become twisted into idolatry. Our conversion experience, our experience of the deeper working of the Holy Spirit can become an idol. We can be living in history instead of in a daily walk with the Living Christ. We can be constantly exploring the archives, remembering past intellectual and spiritual discoveries, worshiping what happened back at a certain date and time; forgetting that that was only to be a starting point.

Have you ever seen a person spend all his time reminding people of his birthdate? "I was born physically on June 8, 1921." What a great day for you and the world! That person will die of malnutrition if he isn't living now; physically eating, drinking, sleeping, involving himself in human dynamic relationships. The same thing applies spiritually. Thank God for your conversion experience, for your experience with the Lord. But don't let that date in time become your idol. Don't let that previous spiritual experience block you from a today relationship with the God who has new things he wants to do with you and your life.

Our idolatry can extend also to an individual church. You love your congregation. You've come to know Christ through its ministry. Something happens that you leave your community in which that congregation is based. You don't know how you will survive. Someone told me recently, "If I would have to leave Pittsburgh, I just don't see how I would grow spiritually. I know I'll never again find a church like ours." That's inflating to the minister's ego; we love to hear things like that about our church. Granted, we understand the closeness of affection one can develop for a home church. Yet idolatry is idolatry. A church which comes front and center as the contact point with God can quickly become a graven image, an idol, if it's only through that church one can grow in relationship with God. That's the curse called institutionalization. The structure which should provide a vehicle for spiritual expression can itself become the end.

Thus far, we've mentioned only religious objects and experiences that can become idols. You probably were expecting elaborate conversation about material objects. Not only can we give the wrong kind of worship to the right God, we can do something far more serious. We can give the right kind of worship to the wrong gods. In her book *Smoke on the Mountain,* Joy Davidman writes:

> I worship my Lincoln Continental. All my days I give it offerings of oil and polish. Hours of my time are devoted to its care. It establishes me among my neighbors as a success in life. What model is your car, brother?
>
> I worship my beautiful house. Long and loving meditation have I spent on it. The upholstery contrasts with the rugs, and the curtains harmonize with the paint—all of it is perfect and

holy. The Dresden figurines and antique knick-knacks are in exactly the right places; and should some blasphemer drop ashes on the carpet, I nearly die of shock. I live for the adoration of my house, and it rewards me with the envy of my neighbors who rise up and call me artistic. Lest my children profane the shrine of my home with dirt and noise, I put them out of doors. What condition is your house in, sister?

I worship my job. . . . I worship my clothes. . . . I worship my golf game. . . . I worship my comfort. . . . I worship my Church: I want to tell you that the quality of our congregation beats all others in this town!

I worship myself!

Now, what shape is your idol? [1]

The Second Commandment says that God is a jealous God who doesn't want anything to get between us and him. He doesn't want interference even if it's good interference. What he wants is direct contact with every one of us.

Jealousy seems so unreasonable, in person-to-person relationships. Perhaps you're offended that God would label himself "jealous." Perhaps we have a distorted understanding. Jealousy isn't the unreasonableness and cruelty with which we so often equate it. God's jealousy is not that of a sadistic husband who tries to hem his wife in by cutting off her contacts with the outside world. His jealousy is pure. It is simply caring for us. We can't get jealous of something to which we are indifferent. God is jealous of our affection. It hurts him when we neglect his loving statement "I am the Lord your God." He wants an exclusive relationship, with no competition or interference. He says, "You shall not make for yourself a graven image or any likeness of anything that is in heaven about or that is in the earth beneath or that is in the water under the earth. You shall not bow down to them or serve them for I the Lord your God am a jealous God. . . ."

He doesn't want us creating substitutes for him. When we do it, it grieves his heart, and he wants us back. He wants to shower us with his affection, and he wants our love in return. He does not want us to destroy ourselves by serving the creature instead of the Creator.

It's interesting to note how God responds to our various attitudes toward him.

Idolatry's price is expensive for us and future generations. God says that he visits the iniquity of the fathers upon the children to the third and the fourth generations of those who hate him. That sounds harsh. He's saying that evil has its rewards. Idolatry leads to debasement. The person who does not worship in simple faith hurts future generations. Children pick up our values in the home. Heredity and environment make their impact. Sophisticated tolerance is dangerous. The person who does not respond in love and true worship, who lets other things get in the way, hurts future innocent generations. This does not negate God's love. He still loves us and our children. He wants to release us from the visitations of unhappiness which we communicate to our children and our children's children when things get between us and God.

Even as idolatry produces pain for us and future generations, love and obedience produce mercy. True worship has its rewards. The person who is honest and simple in his or her faith, who worships the one God who has revealed himself in the risen Christ, finds blessing for him or herself and future generations. God says that he shows steadfast love to thousands of those who love him and keep his commandments. God's mercy is greater than anything else. His father love in Jesus Christ covers a multitude of sins and releases us into the fullest life possible, free from guilt and man-made depression.

When all is said, idolatry is simply your effort and mine to tame God. How we try to twist him into our mold! We can't do that to God. Instead of asking him to rearrange his life around us, why not let God be first and then rearrange our life around him. Allow him to chip away at our idols. Allow Jesus Christ to stand foremost as Savior and Lord. No one else and nothing else need get in the way!

*"You shall not take the name of the Lord your God in vain; for the Lord will not hold him guiltless who takes his name in vain."*
*Exodus 20:7*

# 4.
# TAKING GOD'S NAME IN VAIN

THIS straightforward commandment tells us what not to do and states our guilt when we disobey. But what does God mean when he says that we shall not take his name in vain? How does this relate to where you and I live today?

The first thing that comes to mind is profanity. You and I could fill a glossary with four-letter words. However, it's not the words themselves that are wrong; it's the irreverent attitude expressed by those words. According to Webster, profanity is that tendency to treat something that is sacred with abuse, irreverence, or contempt. Profanity is the desecration or violation of that which is sacred.

You and I disobey this divine command when we engage in profanity, when we use God's name to spice up our conversation, when God's name takes the place of our punctuation marks. Recently there was a cartoon that showed a secretary speaking to her boss. He had just commended her on a fine manuscript she had typed. She responded, "I'm glad you like it, sir. All I did was correct your grammar, rephrase the sentences, change your terminology, omit the profanity, and type it up!"

For many, profanity has become a lifestyle. It's so easy to absorb this from one's associations. Television, the newspapers, everyday office banter bombard the subconscious mind with words that can unwittingly become part of our own vocabulary. An early example of this came in my own life when I was twelve years old. My Arlington, Massachusetts, sixth-grade class had traveled to Fenway Park in Boston to see the Red Sox play and we had sat in the outfield bleachers within earshot of a few Fenway Park regulars who got their kicks from shouting obscenities at Ted Williams. Later that week I was playing some sandlot ball with my friends. A few girls were watching us, among them one I wanted to impress. I struck out! The stream of profanity that failure triggered from my lips shocked both me and my friends. We're so susceptible to environmental influence.

Some use profanity in their desire to impress. A young man with insecure feelings about himself can swagger with bravado, flaunting the name of God, using it to shock. His attempt to grab attention really represents pygmy-size man grabbing hold of God, then pulling him down to our size.

Dwight L. Moody said, "I do not believe men would have been guilty of swearing unless God had forbidden it." There's something in you and me which wants to build our towers of Babel. We want to be gods. We seem to think the way to do this is to utter profanities which reduce the grandeur of a holy God.

Even without God's command, profanity makes little sense. As my sixth-grade teacher (who, incidentally, didn't hear my outburst) used to say, "The person who uses profanity is signaling to the world that he has a small vocabulary." The profane person often is inarticulate, not knowing how to express himself in suitable language.

The use of profanity can also be a sign that the user lacks emotional control. The stable person doesn't need to fly off the handle with oaths that try to call down God's wrath upon the one with whom he's angry. From a purely secular perspective, profanity is futile, subject to diminishing returns. The first few times a person swears, people may perk up their ears. When profanity becomes part of one's normal conversation, it registers nothing in the ears of the person who knows the user. And a person who meets him for the first time quickly gets his number and fails to be impressed.

There's another dimension beyond the secular that should make us very careful in our use of God's name: profanity is ultimately a prayer. If we sprinkle through our conversation the name of God, the name of Jesus Christ, expressions such as "God damn you," or "Go to hell," whether we realize it or not, we are actually mouthing prayers. If taken seriously by God, these have extreme, eternal implications for us and for those to whom we utter them so lightly. Watch out! God may just answer one of those prayers. If you don't mean it, don't say it. But, thanks be to him, he has the eternal wisdom to hold back and give us a chance to clean up our language.

Perhaps you may be taking his name in vain by using it casually in your conversation. It is surprising what inroads this carelessness is making into many a Christian's vocabulary. You may never have taken this issue seriously. Aren't there much worse sins? This seems awfully petty. But hold your surprise for a moment. Get out your Bible. Leaf through it from cover to cover. You'll be amazed at how much there is all the way through the Bible that warns about blasphemy. God would surely not have devoted one of his Ten Commandments to such a topic if he had considered it trite. The Bible says, "The Lord will not hold him guiltless who takes his name in vain." Jesus restated this: "I tell you, on the day of judgment men will render account for every careless word they utter; for by your words you will be justified, and by your words you will be condemned" (Matt. 12:36–37).

Our words are important.

There are additional dimensions to this great commandment that apply to each of us no matter how chaste our lips may be. Have you and I ever stopped to consider that we take God's name in vain when we allow it to be empty of deep personal meaning? You and I can blaspheme not only by what we say, but by what we do and the attitudes we convey. Casualness with spiritual matters is a second way in which we take God's name in vain.

God's name is precious. God's name has depth. God says, "You shall not take the name of the Lord your God in vain. . . ." His name is not to be used tritely. The Septuagint translates this verse to read, "Thou shalt not take the name of Jehovah, thy God, upon a vain or frivolous pretext." God warns against our handling lightly his Word. "I have not sent them, says the Lord, but they are prophesying falsely in my name, with the result that I will drive you out and you will perish, you and the prophets who are prophesying to you" (Jer. 27:15).

Examine closely the Hebrew meaning for "in vain." It means literally "to take up for unreality," to use "falsely," or, "to make use of for any idle, frivolous or insincere purpose."

To the Hebrews a person's name was an essential part of that person's personality. A name was not just a word that stood for a person. The name *was* that person. What was true for an ordinary human being was especially true for God. His name was to be spoken with reverence. His name demanded awe. Jesus underlined this when he taught his disciples to pray saying: "Our Father who art in heaven, hallowed be thy name" (Matt. 6:9).

God's name is sacred. It is set apart; it is holy. Using God's name frequently in a genuine outpouring of spiritual life is right, but it must never be merely a sentimental phrasing of empty cliches. You reverence your mother's name; in fact, you've probably never addressed her by her first name. What would you think of a person who went around using her name in oaths when he or she was upset, startled, or wanted to express hatred? You respect your mother too much to do that. Why then treat God's name so?

There are still more ways in which we take his name in vain. How easy it is for us to take the great truths of God's love in Jesus Christ and use them in ways that lack rich meaning. We talk about the "blood of Jesus Christ" when we have lost the sense of the efficacy of that blood poured out for the remission of our sins. How easy it is to speak of the "fatherhood of God" when we are out of fellowship or in rebellion against this One who loves us and gave himself for us. How easily we champion the brotherhood of man when we know that we're concerned more for "Number One." We're not so interested in our brother who is poor, our brother who is sick, our brother who is emotionally disturbed, our brother who is caught up in crime, our brother who doesn't know God's love.

You and I say together the Apostles' Creed and the Lord's Prayer. When was the last time we repeated those words with real devotional intensity? This is the prayer Christ taught us to pray. It is divinely inspired. The Apostles' Creed is a theological formulation that contains the very heart of the Christian faith.

How easy it is to recite our glib or formal prayers. How quickly we respond to the questions asked of the congregation at the time of baptism. If our church is one that practices infant baptism, do we even remember the names of those youngsters for whom we have taken vows?

What good is orthodox teaching without true spirituality? How quickly my sermons can become mechanical, or worse, become vehicles for self-glory. How often is our confession made without a stricken conscience and our acceptance of God's grace without an inner joy?

Taking God's name in vain involves being casual about our

personal relationship with him. How do we really feel about being a church member? We took vows. Are we following through? We've made commitments. Are we faithful to them? When a Broadway producer offered a well-known actress a part in a new play, the actress was pleased but said, "First, I must consult my horoscope." The producer said, "I didn't know you believed in astrology." The actress answered, "I believe in everything—a little bit." Is that the way we believe in God—a little bit? Is God just one more item included in the safe that houses our valuables? Is he placed in there alongside our commitment to our country, friends, alma mater, and apple pie? Or, is he the transcendent God who makes all of these other commitments subordinate to our one great allegiance to him?

Some of us blaspheme God by our endeavors to prop him up. Not so many people trust him today. Many are inclined to live lives independent of him. In our effort to convince the world he exists, we use gimmicks like slogans and bumper stickers.

His survival doesn't depend on you or me. He's given us tasks to carry out. We are to be faithful. All too often our lifestyle denies the confidence we express when we sing, "He's got the whole world in His hands." Vital Christianity demands a concentration which brings dynamic spiritual living into direct confrontation with spiritual sentimentality, cold orthodoxy, or flippancy.

We take God's name in vain when we profess to be what we really are not. Not only is that profanity and casualness, it's also hypocrisy. There are two particular ways in which our hypocrisy causes us to break this commandment.

One is when we profess to be telling the truth when we are not. In a law court, this is called perjury. In everyday experience, it's called shading the truth. God says, "And you shall not swear by my name falsely, and so profane the name of your God: I am the Lord" (Lev. 19:12). Some have interpreted this Scripture to mean that a Christian should not place his hand on a Bible and swear in the name of God that he is telling the truth. Actually it means that no one should swear in God's name that he's telling the truth and then deliberately lie. As believers, we are called to truthfulness.

Society must be built on two foundational supports. One is the love of truth. The other is the fear of God. There is no way that a society can maintain the high standard called truth unless there is a deep fear of God. He is truth. Out of him comes all truth.

A second form of hypocrisy is to bear the name *Christian* when we don't meet the qualifications. Have you ever received Jesus Christ as your Savior? Do you acknowledge him as your Lord? No, I'm not talking about following him as the great example. I'm not talking about the ethical idealism called Christianity. I'm not talking about an inherited faith that bases its credentials on the fact that your mother, grandmother, and great-grandmother were all Presbyterians, or Methodists, or some other denomination, therefore you are a Christian.

In a church I formerly served as pastor, one of the most demanding functions assigned to me and the Session was to meet with people who wished to join our congregation. We could very rapidly have increased our membership if we had opened wide the doors to all who expressed the desire to join by transfer of letter, taking for granted that they were Christians. Many were quite surprised to find that they were asked to meet personally with one of the pastors and then appear before the Session. It would have been much easier simply to receive their letters and place them on the membership rolls, but by our requirements we were calling them to examine at a deep level the seriousness of their commitment. It was not our desire to appear judgmental; we simply felt we would be doing a severe disservice to many persons who think they are

Christians but have never really professed Jesus Christ as their Savior. No human being is to be the judge, of course, and God's Word stands as the only infallible rule of faith and practice. But God's Word clearly indicates which persons are Christians. These are the persons who bear God's name. These are persons who bow before him in absolute allegiance.

Peter stood before the Jewish leaders in Jerusalem. With all his background in the Jewish scriptures, he declared:

> "... Be it known to you all, and to all the people of Israel, that by the name of Jesus Christ of Nazareth, whom you crucified, whom God raised from the dead, by him this man is standing before you well. This is the stone which was rejected by you builders, but which has become the head of the corner. And there is salvation in no one else, for there is no other name under heaven given among men by which we must be saved" (Acts 4: 10–12).

The Apostle Paul expressed a similar thought as he expressed Christ's divinity:

> Therefore God has highly exalted him and bestowed on him the name which is above every name, that at the name of Jesus every knee should bow, in heaven and on earth and under the earth, and every tongue confess that Jesus Christ is Lord, to the glory of God the Father (Phil. 2: 9–11).

It is at the name of Jesus that every knee should bow. If you have received Jesus Christ and are growing as a Christian, to you his name is a name filled with awe. It is identical with divine majesty. It is a name you will want to exalt, a name you will want to share. The name of Jesus does not provide primarily a nice success formula for living. The name of Jesus does not stand only as a symbol of good productive living. The name of Jesus is not meant to provide respectability in the community. The name of Jesus Christ is God become man in human form. It is a miracle. In this incarnation, God has shed his blood for the remission of your sins. He has risen from the dead in triumph. To treat Jesus Christ in anything less than exalted worship is spiritual libel. It's to use his name falsely.

You are not forced to profess him. If you do, it had better be for real. Big men in secular society go to great ends to protect their names. They correct injustices by suing for libel. God goes to great ends to protect the integrity of his personality which offers us salvation. Perhaps it's time for you to either "fish or cut bait." Either you are a Christian or you are not. The issue is not some debate about science and the Scripture. It's not conversation about denominationalism. It's not playing games over economic and political theory. We are here to proclaim the name of Jesus Christ and call others to faith in him. You are taking God's name in vain if you're professing to be a Christian when you are not.

This isn't particularly a pleasant message, is it? You and I are wedged in from three angles. We take God's name in vain by our profanity, by our casualness, and by our hypocrisy. Our text says that God will not hold us guiltless who take his name in vain. Each one of us is responsible to him.

There is, however, an exciting positive aspect. As you and I commit ourselves to Christ in faith, expose ourselves to daily growth in Christian living, we have the refreshing, uplifting, invigorating, spiritual energizing that comes through God's free gift called grace. Our sins are forgiven, not on the basis of what we've done, but on the basis of what Christ has done for us. The best way to be sure we're not profaning his name is to be in daily contact with him. We can have a romance with One who wants us to honor his name. When we have this relation-

ship, this deep parent-child love, our very spiritual nature cries
out against blasphemy.

The Puritan preacher Thomas Watson related this story.[1]
There was a woman who admitted to her husband that of her
three sons only one was his. The father, who lay dying, did not
want his inheritance to go to the two illegitimate children who
bore his name. So he asked the executors of his estate to find
out which was the true, natural son. Then he instructed them
to bequeath all his assets to him. After the father died, the
executors used a strange method to ascertain which was the
true son. They set the father's corpse against a tree. They gave
to each of the three sons a bow and a quiver of arrows telling
them that he who could shoot nearest the father's heart should
have the whole estate. Two sons shot as near as they could to
his heart. But the third felt nature so at work in him that he
refused to shoot, whereupon the executors judged him to be the
true son and gave him all the estate.

The true children of God fear to shoot at him. Those who
are bastards and not sons feel free to shoot at him with arrows
and curses. If we are true children of God we will hold him in
awe and reverence in our speech. Our attitude of life, our profession of faith will not allow us to shoot at the Father's
heart.

"Remember the sabbath day, to keep it holy. Six days shall you labor and do all your work; but the seventh day is a sabbath to the Lord your God; in it you shall not do any work. . . ."

*Exodus 20:8–10*

# 5.

# WHAT GOD HAS TO SAY ABOUT TAKING A DAY OFF

Do YOU remember the Sabbath day to keep it holy? What is your immediate reaction to that point-blank question?

Perhaps it takes you back to your childhood and your reaction against a severe interpretation of this command. Your parents were extremely strict about what you could and couldn't do on Sunday. No Sunday newspaper. No sports. No purchases at those few stores that did stay open. Yours was a youth filled with "blue laws."

I've a friend who is deeply resentful of his strict upbringing. Every Sunday there was Sunday school, church, youth fellowship and the evening service. According to his account, the most exciting thing he was allowed to do between these services was to sit on the front porch and listen to his hair grow. If he really wanted to get brazen, he and his brothers, on the sly, would count the out-of-state license plates on passing automobiles.

That's one extreme—a very negative approach to Sunday. Did you come from this kind of background? You may be in reaction. You may be expecting me to bombard you with pietistic talk telling you what you can and can't do on Sunday.

Or perhaps you come at this from the other extreme. To you Sunday is not that much different from any other day. When someone asks you, "Do you remember the Sabbath day to keep it holy?" your reaction probably is: "What in the world are you talking about? I go to church when I can. Isn't that enough?" Some of us come from backgrounds that treat all seven days pretty much equal. We're aware that there is something called the Sabbath. The Jews celebrated it on the seventh day, our Saturday. Then there is Sunday, the Christian day. You go to church and that's it.

God says in his Fourth Commandment:

> Remember the sabbath day, to keep it holy. Six days you shall labor, and do all your work; but the seventh day is a sabbath to the Lord your God; in it you shall not do any work, you, or your son, or your daughter, your manservant, or your cattle, or the so-journer who is within your gates; for in six days the Lord made heaven and earth, the sea, and all that is in them, and rested the seventh day; therefore the Lord blessed the sabbath day and hallowed it (Exod. 20: 8–11).

There is a difference between the Sabbath and Sunday. The Old Testament Jew observed the Sabbath. It literally means "rest day." Another way of putting it is that it is a "stop-what you-are-doing day," a twenty-four–hour period set aside for rest and restoration. I particularly like the way Arthur Sueltz writes about it in his book entitled *New Directions from the Ten Commandments*. He describes how he needs regular "time-outs." Without them all the happiness and joy drains out of his existence. Yet he says, time gets away from him. Instead of spending the hours of his own life, others spend them for him. So he says, Sabbath means "I need time out. Time out to take eternity in. Time when I stop doing what I usually do."[1] The Sabbath reminds you that you're made for something bigger than working yourself to death or running yourself to death for fear you might miss something.

Sunday is a little bit different. As you know, the Hebrews observed the Sabbath from sundown Friday to sundown Saturday. It was the seventh day. The early Christian church introduced a different day. It was a Sunday celebration. It happened on the first day of the week, which was an ordinary working day for both Jews and Gentiles. We forget that the first Christians didn't get Sunday off. They gathered before or after work to celebrate Christ's resurrection. There was a major difference between a Sabbath rest and restoration and Sunday worship. Ultimately, as society became more and more influenced by Christianity, Sunday became the day set aside for both rest and worship. Now, with a five-day work week most of us are able to have a day set aside for each of these specific purposes.

My task is not to be legalistic, calling for a return to some previous era of Sabbath observance. Jesus blatantly broke some of those 1,521 types of unlawful Sabbath actions. As he did it, he declared: "The sabbath was made for man, not man for the sabbath; so the Son of man is lord even of the sabbath" (Mark 2:27–28).

He wasn't repudiating the Old Testament commandment. Instead he was attacking its perversion. He was holding two principles in juxtaposition. On the one hand, he was saying, remember the Sabbath. There's a day, one in seven, which must be kept holy. It's a special day. A day for worship. A day to praise God. On the other hand, it's a day which was made by God for you. It's your special day. One out of seven is yours for rest and recreation.

You need at least one full day a week for rest and worship. This command of God frees you to live the most creative life possible. Its rationale is that the human organism—body, mind, and spirit—demands a day of rest. Whether your work is physical or mental, you need rest. Your body needs a time to repose. So does your mind. Your soul, that very being which is uniquely you, created by God, distinct from all other animals, needs a quiet communion with the Lord. Jesus is instructing you today to strip yourself free from legalism, while at the same time he urges you to move beyond the libertarian approach that sees every day as equal. He wants to help keep you from destroying yourself.

First, let's take a look at our need for rest. This is not to minimize the importance of work. Most of the week we work. Work is good if it's restricted to six days. Add one more and there's trouble. The Bible emphasizes that you have a vocation. A job well done is basic to Christianity. At the same time, God's Word is just as quick to say that a person who works hard is a person in whom pressure will build up. If this pressure builds up too far, it will minimize that person's effectiveness. If there's no escape valve, that person will ultimately destroy him or herself. A day off once a week gives release from this pressure. This command is for our good.

I like the word *recreation*. Stop and think about it for a moment. It literally means re-creation. The Bible continually emphasizes the fact that God himself knows the necessity of rest, of re-creation. After his creation, whether one interprets this as a literal six-day period of time or as long eras, he rested.

I've had the funerals of several men who were "workaholics," individuals who literally burned themselves out by overwork. They never learned to relax. They took themselves too seriously. They never realized the fleeting nature of their tasks. Look at the ridiculous "rat race" in which you and I involve ourselves. We press hard to make our profits this year only to be forced to outdo ourselves next year. American life is geared to pressing on with intensity. Read the stories of successful men. You see it repeated time and time again.

Some time ago I read an article about a family in a national magazine. It described this family as being quite different from the ordinary in that the father was not the typical, successful businessman who used his home and family merely as a "psychic service station." The writer described the typical successful American man in these words:

> Mr. America, it seemed to us (and what with deadlines and travel assignments, we could afford no smugness), is a visitor to his home, and his "success" in the world generally is measured by the shortness of his visits.

> How many of those cover stories have you read in the newsmagazines? Formal and predictable, they sing of Mr. Executive, who has transformed Omnipex Electronics from a pennyante gadget shop to a corporate entity intent on gobbling its competitive way around half the globe. Or Mr. Statesman, who is ushered through a truly incredible day that begins at dawn with coffee and communiques in bed, and ends, after the state dinner, with a "second day" at the office. About two-thirds into the story, you sense a slight shift in tone as a cardboard family is rolled onstage. There is a mercifully brief recounting of the idyllic courtship, the lean and loyal early years, the arrival of the heirs; and then the wife is allowed a sentence or two. Rueful but proud, she affirms her role as the humble handmaiden of Success, and drops out of sight as the story moves on to its justification-for-practically-anything: Manly Service to Others.

> But another message squeezes up between the words: perhaps these corporate and public servants would do better to serve not "others" but themselves and their families. They rarely do anything to enrich our lives, because they have not enriched their own. And what can justify the unjelled, resentful children they loose like a plague on the world?

How about it? How about you, Mr. Businessman? How about you, Mr. Doctor? How about you, Mrs. Housewife? How about you, Ms. Careerwoman? How about me, Mr. Minister? Have we become so busy that we've forgotten how to live? Have our lives become so plastic in their success that we fail to realize the necessity for rest, for that re-creation of body, mind, and spirit which makes us the whole people God has created us to be?

In my estimation, a person who will not relax and rest suffers from an ego that is out of control. He or she may not be aware of this. But what that person really is saying is, "I am indispensable. I must be on top of things all the time or my business can't succeed. My profession will not be what it should be. My ministry will fail." It's amazing how quickly those shoes are filled when he or she drops dead from overwork. That is, the shoes are filled almost instantly for everyone except the widow and children.

What the Bible is talking about is not a call to laziness but to a perspective that sees the importance of pacing oneself. Some of the most productive people I know have mastered this principle and learned to pace themselves over the long haul in a balanced way. Have you ever watched the long-distance runner begin a marathon race of close to twenty-seven miles? That runner doesn't sprint the first hundred yards. The goal is the long haul, not the short dash. The runner starts out slowly, plodding on with the consistency of measured pace, not caring how many get ahead in the beginning since many of them will fall back along the way.

Isn't that what we all want? Physical, intellectual, social, spiritual equipment for the long-distance run? We can't stay vigorous in each of these areas if we disregard our need for rest.

Doctors, students, ministers, and mothers are some of the biggest offenders in this area. As a pastor, I wish I had the guts to physically shake some of the doctors I know who spend all of their time dealing with the physical needs of others, not realizing what they're doing to themselves by not getting proper rest and recreation. They need a day off every week.

We come to church and sing piously, "O day of rest and gladness." If we truly concentrated on the words, it would be amusing to the typical mother who has managed the washing, dressing, and feeding of children; preparation of Sunday dinner; and departure for church early enough to arrive on time. Somehow we have to figure out a way to give a Sabbath to a wife and mother.

We ministers are probably the greatest chronic offenders. Many of my colleagues pride themselves on the fact that they never take a day off. One told me that this was the biggest mistake he ever made. He gave everything he had to his first church to the point that he drove himself to physical exhaustion and a breakdown of health; that in turn pushed his wife and son to nervous breakdowns. How many others I've seen zealously working seven days a week who ended up getting all of those missed days off together in one batch as they recuperated from a heart attack. The principle is clear.

We need one day off in seven for rest, for re-creation. If, like me, you have to work on Sunday, make it on Monday or a Saturday. Part of my calling as a pastor who takes the Word of God seriously is to observe a Sabbath—a day of rest. That's why, unless there's a wedding or severe emergency, I jealously guard my Saturdays. And if I have to miss one, I faithfully make it up. One person said the human body is a seven-day clock. If it is not rewound every seventh day, it will ultimately run itself down into the grave.

I thank God that I learned this lesson early in life. During college and seminary, I worked in the travel business. In 1959 I met Dr. and Mrs. Norman Vincent Peale and their family while they were vacationing in Jerusalem. Out of this came plans for large group travel to the Holy Land. In 1961 and 1962 it was my responsibility to handle all the travel arrangements for pilgrimages averaging 150 people in number. I worked hard at this. In 1963, as well as assisting him at Marble Collegiate Church in New York, I led a tour around the world for Dr. Peale. As we traveled through the Far East and then through India, my health began to fail. Finally, by the time we got to New Delhi I was plagued by exhaustion, a bad cold, and dysentery. For nine years, during high school, college, and the first year of seminary, I had burned the candle at both ends. I'll never forget Dr. Peale and an industrialist friend of his getting me alone in a corner and giving me some of the best advice I ever received. It capsules everything I've been trying to share from God's Word in this chapter. "The way you're going now, you're starting out in life like a skyrocket firecracker, but the pace you're keeping will cause you to fizzle out in the next ten or fifteen years," they said. "Take it from us veterans of the long haul, pace yourself. Take a day off. Get the proper change of environment. You may not go quite so far so fast, but you'll be around a lot longer, serving the Christ you love over the next forty, fifty, sixty years."

We need a change of pace. A good clean day off. If your work is mental, have a physical outlet. If your work is physical, do something with your mind. Make that Sabbath different from the other six days, finding rest and recreation. Are you getting your day off? Are you taking time? Do it and don't feel guilty about it. You will have to answer before your God for what you are doing with your time.

Second, not only do we need time for rest and recreation, we need time for worship. The Sabbath is not only for rest, it also is a special time to be with your God.

Work or play must not get in the way of God. Worship is

not to be a painful obligation. It is to be the recharging of one's spiritual batteries. The observance of the Lord's Day promotes our spiritual life. We can't grow in relationship with Christ without it. Business makes us forgetful of God. So can recreation. Proper worship makes the frozen heart melt. Celebrate the union of God and man in the person of Jesus Christ. Celebrate his resurrection from the dead. I'm absolutely amazed at how many who would call themselves Christians neglect their worship privilege. They've learned how to rest. They've reorganized their lives so as to get time to recharge their physical and mental batteries. But what about their spiritual batteries?

I've seen this happen in so many cases over my years in the ministry. Two people start out with great spiritual vitality. They take seriously the biblical admonition to "neglect not the assembling of yourselves together." They are faithful in attending Sunday school and worship services. They involve themselves in their church's corporate life. Over a period of time, they accumulate the financial means to afford that weekend or two away. Finally, they buy a weekend retreat. No, there's nothing wrong with having a place in the country, if factored into that is a disciplined attendance of worship services with other believers who live in that same vicinity. But do you know that's hard to do? A casual attitude develops. The couple rationalizes, "We don't need to go to church every Sunday." So they don't go many Sundays.

Whereas, if we miss a meal, we get hungry, the opposite is the case when it comes to spiritual matters. Miss church a few times and hunger for Christian fellowship decreases. You feel your need less and less. And there's an especially tragic spin-off. You produce children who get the message. No, not the message you intended, but the one you're really communicating.

They grow up to take the things of God casually. They miss Christian fellowship. You'll find them indifferent to spiritual matters.

Now, yours may not be a weekend retreat cabin. It may be professional football. Frankly, I'm as avid a Pittsburgh Steeler fan as you'll find. Some would say that a Christian shouldn't attend a professional football game on Sunday. It seems to me that this, along with other Sabbath practices, is up to a person's own conscience. But when professional football becomes one's god, there's spiritual trouble in store.

Some time ago, a minister in Green Bay, Wisconsin, preached a sermon titled "God and the Green Bay Packers." He said,

> On Autumn Sundays everyone's schedule—every family's, every church's—is determined by the playing schedule of the Green Bay Packers. It is obvious that the most sacred period of the week is the time when the Packers play. . . . My criticism is largely a criticism of emphasis.

Ron Hudspeth wrote in the *Atlanta Journal-Constitution:*

> This is dedicated to the pro football generation. Call it Social Sunday. Religion of the Seventies. Worship of a 250-pound idol in cleats and athletic supporter.
>
> It is a few minutes past eleven on a gray Sunday morning in Atlanta. A church bell echoes in the distance. It is heard by only a few. Empty pews dot the beautiful churches on Peachtree Street. There will be no empty seats at Atlanta Stadium.
>
> This Sunday Atlanta Stadium will be quiet. Worship services begin at 4 P.M. from Los Angeles. Via the tube. Rams vs. Falcons. Social Sunday in Absentia.[2]

And Carl Rowan, columnist for Field Enterprises, recently described professional football as our nation's "new religion" for Sundays. "It is, in truth, a microcosm of what the whole society could be like if we could only be as devotedly religious about the rest of life as we are about football."

One of the biggest tragedies we see is the tragedy of a man or a woman who is not exposed to a vital worship of Jesus Christ. Recreation is good, but if we find ourselves getting more excited about our recreation than what God has done for us in Jesus Christ, it's time to confront the fact that we are spiritually sick. We need the drastic therapy called repentance which will shake us out of our distorted priorities back into a proper balance.

Imagine the tragic result that comes from a lack of exposure to the things of God in worship. If you want to be a physical giant, you exercise your body. You lift weights. You eat proper foods. You get good rest. If you want to be a mental giant, you exercise your mind through rigorous academic discipline. If you want to be a social giant, you exercise your personality, developing the skill of interacting with other people. Along the same line, if you have any aspiration to be a spiritual giant, a person at peace with yourself and with your God, you need to exercise your spiritual nature. This is done through worship, on three levels. One is individual worship, which we can find in that solitary moment when our hearts are open to God in prayer and we are faithful in searching the Scriptures. Family worship is basic to this Fourth Commandment also: it is our responsibility to spend time with our families, opening our shared life to the things of God. And then there is public worship, in which we and other believers, persons from all walks of life, unite with each other despite our individual differences to be together under the Lordship of Jesus Christ.

Perhaps your Sunday worship has lost some of its meaning for you. Let me share a couple of brief pointers.

First, prepare for worship. Don't come cold, any more than

you'd tee off on the first hole of a round of golf without at least stretching your arms and swinging the club. Go to bed at a reasonable time Saturday night. Get up early on Sunday morning. Read the Scriptures. Meditate on God's creation, his holiness, his redeeming love in Jesus Christ, and the glory of his promise of eternal life now and in heaven to come. Pray. Pray for the preaching of the Word which will come later in the morning. Pray for yourself that God will convict you where you need conviction. Pray for your pastor that he will speak a message of spiritual power. Pray for others who will come that they will expose themselves in deeper ways to God's love and plan for their lives. Come to the sanctuary prepared, in a spirit of worship. It's amazing what will happen. Regardless of the preacher, preparation will help avoid distractions and drowsiness.

Second, don't mistake verbal eloquence for preaching. Fancy preaching can be like a woman who in vanity paints her face to make it beautiful but neglects her health to the point that disease runs havoc within her body. The best preachers I know are solid, basic, and relevant in their presentation of biblical truth. Eloquence of speech can transport you to heights of understanding of biblical truth. But when it is not grounded in the depths of God's revelation, this eloquence can lead its hearers astray. You and I are here primarily to reach up together to touch the hand of God. Let's not give ourselves up to the worship of architecture, homiletics, and music. One astute observer said, "Some, instead of judging themselves for sin, sit as judges upon the preacher; his sermon had either too much gall in it, or it was too long. They would sooner censure a sermon than practice it. God will judge the judge."

Third, remember that worship involves service. Sunday is not to be an inactive day. Rest and recreation, yes. Private, family and public meditation, yes. But true worship also involves action. Do something. Not because you like to do it. Do it in sacrificial service for God. Teach a Sunday school class. Sing in the choir. Visit a shut-in. Invite a visitor home for dinner.

One final principle: free others as much as possible so that they too can observe the Sabbath.

Perhaps you expected me to lash out against the stores being opened on Sundays. I am opposed to the department stores being open on Sunday. I wish that we lived in a society in which everybody could celebrate Sunday as his or her day off. I wish we lived in a society where right and wrong were much more clearly understandable than in ours. However, as long as the corner drugstore can sell cosmetics, as long as the filling station can sell automotive parts, I can see why the department stores insist on their right to fair competition. But it's a vicious circle. When they open, they put pressure on smaller stores whose employees may not get a day off.

This doesn't mean that we have to participate in a pagan effort to make Sunday just one more ordinary day exactly like the other six. We can set some disciplines for ourselves in which we do only that work which is absolutely necessary and arrange to do our purchasing in advance. Jesus acknowledged that people had to feed their animals on the Sabbath. He also noted that emergencies had to be handled. One Christian was urged by his employer to work on Sunday. The employer said, "Doesn't your Bible tell you that Jesus said if your ass falls into a pit on the Sabbath, you may pull him out?" "Yes," the Christian responded, "but if the ass had a habit of falling into the same pit every Sabbath, I would either fill up the pit, or sell the ass."

Watch out for exploitation. Some of us have influence over a large number of people. You and I are responsible to protect that one day out of seven, assuring that those persons are not exploited. See that they are given the proper time off so that they can have rest, recreation, and time for worship.

How about you? Are you remembering the Sabbath day to keep it holy, providing the rest and spiritual refreshment both you and your fellowmen need?

"Honor your father and your mother, that your days may be long in the land which the Lord your God gives you."
*Exodus 20:12*

# 6.

# FOR CHILDREN OF ALL AGES

HOW SAD it is to observe a rebellious child. He thinks he knows more than his father. Perhaps he does. He scorns his mother's simple values. Pride drives him forward. In scorn he looks down on those who brought him into this world, who gave him his start.

God pity the society led by brash young people who have all the answers but very little respect for their elders. Anarchy comes quickly. Allow young people to be alienated from their parents and you'll observe a nation drift into moral and social anarchy. Family life is crucial to a healthy society. Children who grab hold of the household reins, pushing their parents aside, inflict a serious damage on society. Young people who grow up without subjection to authority are programming themselves for unhappiness. A society as well as an individual pays an enormous price for weakening the honor paid to fathers and mothers.

God knows this. He understands that living is tough. He's aware that contemporary living gets faster and faster. He saw it happen some three thousand plus years ago to the Jewish people. For four hundred years they had said, "Yes, master," in a dehumanizing slave relationship to their Egyptian masters. Suddenly the lid popped off. They were liberated and led into freedom by Moses. No longer could anyone treat them as slaves.

A crisis develops. It's a crisis in authority. New guidance is needed. Will these people be able to survive a forty-year wilderness trek? God knows they can, but it won't be easy. So God, through Moses, gives instructions. Tersely stated, they are the Ten Commandments. The first four instruct the Jews—and, in turn, instruct us—how to get along with God. They deal with vertical God-man relationships. Then God shifts gears. The next six commandments deal with person-to-person relationships. The emphasis is on the horizontal.

It's no accident that the Fifth Commandment, the first one dealing with horizontal relationships, starts with the human family. God is convinced that the human family must never break down. Not long ago the late Margaret Mead predicted that within forty years the family would be out of date. Other sociologists prophesy the breakdown of the family, among them Carle C. Zimmerman of Harvard University: "The Western family is rapidly approaching its third violent crisis. This crisis will be the third manifestation of mass disregard of the family in Western society. . . . The first occurred in Greece, the second in Rome, and facing these crises neither Greek nor Roman civilization was able to survive."[1]

You're aware of the problem. Our young people are experiencing an entirely different social conditioning from that of previous generations. Our time was spent in the home, the church, the school, and community activities. Life was lived with a greater leisure. Family spirit was important. Now our young people are exposed to subtle, and some not-so-subtle, forms of manipulation that twist them away from substantial family living.

Television, with all of its positive potential, drives a wedge into meaningful family conversation. The average child between kindergarten and graduation from high school spends 11,000 hours in a classroom. During the same period of years, that same child will spend 15,000 hours in front of a television set. It is not unusual for a one-minute commercial to cost between $100,000 to $200,000. Imagine the high-quality psychological, artistic, sociological engineering that goes into that expensive salesmanship. Even when we're together in front of a television set, we can sit as if encased in individualistic capsules incapable of communicating with each other.

Television isn't the only culprit. Life just moves so fast. One comments, "Has family life any real riches any more? No wonder many young boys and girls are delinquent. They have no home lives. They eat out of the refrigerator. The members of the family keep different hours. They leave notes for one another."

I'm not laying the blame on our youth for the social anarchy we are facing, nor am I asking for a return to a previous era. I *am* emphasizing the biblical answer to our nation's problem— there's no substitute for godly parents and a godly home. Young people who are not reared in an environment in which they sense the love of God within the framework of the human family are going to react in negative behavior patterns. This behavior is the outgrowth of the distrust of self, family, and society. Talk to law enforcement agents. Talk to ministers. Talk to educators. Talk to sociologists, psychiatrists, and psychologists. Most of them will single out the lack of parental control as being the primary factor in the unrest we are facing today. There are other factors, of course, and we must be grateful for the many young people who are sensitized to social and ethical concerns. We can be proud of young people who are willing to be critics of our society, who are willing to make moral evaluations of our domestic and foreign involvements. The question is one of attitude. How can we preserve our homes? How should the young person respond to parental authority?

It's to this very point that God speaks through Moses, to ancient Israel and to us today. He gives it in the way of a command, the disobedience of which will wreak havoc on individual, family, social, and national life. Its obedience, on the other hand, will bring constructive revolution to each of these areas. The command reads simply, "Honor your father and your mother, that your days may be long in the land which the Lord your God gives you" (Exod. 20:12).

You and I are to honor our parents. Honor means that we attach weight to what they say, put them in the place of superiority, hold them high in our opinion. We are to reverence them in the best sense of the term. When you and I hold our parents in this kind of esteem, a respect mingled with love results and breeds an environment that can be passed on to the next generation. In fact, a healthy reverence for father and mother lies at the basis of all morality.

I realize that to many, this sounds sort of old-fashioned. We live in a youth-oriented culture. Gray hairs which once symbolized wisdom are dyed to a more youthful color. Nubile feminine bodies matched with virile young masculine frames dressed in the latest and most expensive fashions sell our products. Occasionally, a grandfatherly type is pictured, but he is usually caricatured. Today is owned by the young.

There's even a tendency in modern psychology to blame parents for our mistakes. This tendency is both good and bad. It's good in that some of our youthful problems are inherited. The sin of one generation is passed on. Until we see the source of our problems, we are helpless to cope with them. On the other hand, this modern tendency to blame our parents for everything which goes wrong is bad. Why?

It's bad because it helps us escape blame for our irresponsible actions. Children, isn't it convenient to blame your parents for everything you do wrong? That way you don't have to assume responsibility. But that failure to assume responsibility is a classic sign of one's immaturity. It's only when we're able to face up to the reality of our own mistakes that we are mature persons.

Blaming our parents for our problems is bad because it ultimately makes us hate ourselves. Deep within us we know that there's no perfect parent. All of us have valid resentments. At the same time, those of us in the business of parenting children know we're no more perfect than our parents. If we spend too much time pinning blame on them, we become all the more aware that our own children will have good reason to pin some on us. If we'll stop long enough to think about it and admit it, we can see that we too are making our mistakes and passing them on to another generation.

The tendency to blame our parents is bad also because it can destroy our relationships with them. If we allow ourselves to become too critical of the previous generation, we will find ourselves facing an emotional separation from our parents. And that alienation will ultimately prove so expensive.

Here are two biblical models. Study them at your leisure. Look how differently these children handled relationships with problem parents who made their mistakes.

One is Absalom. He had every reason in the world to rebel against his father, David. David had several wives. He was an absentee father who was usually at war or busy ruling his people. But when Absalom did rebel, he paid the price. Have you ever observed a rebel son or daughter who has lived a happy life? It doesn't work. We can't cut ourselves off from our roots and be fulfilled persons.

Another model is Joseph. His father, Jacob, didn't do everything right. He manipulated people. He had lied to get his way. He had shown favoritism which inadvertently encouraged his eleven other sons to hate Joseph. They couldn't stand their spoiled brother who had that fancy robe and dreamed himself superior. So they sold him into slavery. His lot in Egypt was tough. Accused of doing something he didn't do, he ended up in prison. But then the breaks went his way and he became the greatest man in Egypt, next to Pharaoh. The nation bowed before him as he wore the finest garments. The court psychiatrists could have told him how fortunate it was that he had gotten away from his father. Now he could be mature, his own man. So different from Absalom, Joseph wasn't satisfied until he had brought his father to Egypt. Whereas Absalom died holding his father in contempt, Joseph hurried out to meet Jacob. He refused to be ashamed of the now destitute old man wearing the shepherd's clothes.

We parents should do our best to be worthy of honor. There's no excuse for us to exploit our children. How many a child has been driven to distraction by a doting mother or a nonaccepting father. The Apostle Paul saw this tendency in some of us. He wrote, "Fathers, do not provoke your children to anger, but bring them up in the discipline and instruction of the Lord" (Eph. 6:4). Nonetheless, there's no excuse for our treating our parents in anything less than full honor, full reverence.

Two specific obligations of this Fifth Commandment stand out.

First, we are to obey our parents. Colossians 3:20 makes clear, "Children, obey your parents in everything, for this pleases the Lord." Granted, there is a day when we leave home and are on our own. The Bible says the young man is to leave his father and mother and cling to his wife. He will not always be obligated to obedience. I think the rule of thumb on this kind of careful obedience is that as long as a person is under their roof and/or is receiving their support, he or she has a responsibility to obey them. Accept their authority, even if there is disagreement with their thinking.

Obviously, there will be times when parents will give advice in the spirit of "take it or leave it, this is my opinion." There will be times when they will speak with authority and say, "You do this!" Children may disagree with what their parents are telling them. Yet, I suggest both on the basis of biblical authority and from my own practical experience that if children are going to accept their parents' food, housing, and money, they have the obligation to do what the parents say. Parents have a wisdom that goes beyond the wisdom of their children. And it won't hurt the children one single bit to follow their orders.

In fact, faithful obedience instead of being limiting, actually brings freedom. It frees the young person from responsibility and care until his or her character is framed and mind is trained to develop a correct judgment. Otherwise, the result could be a wrecked life. The older one gets the more responsibility one can assume. Soon enough one will be making all one's own decisions. By then a great deal will have been learned from watching one's parents and living in obedience to them.

Let me add a little footnote at this point. Perhaps you're a young person asking, "What should I do when my parents aren't Christians and don't care that I am? Am I still supposed to obey them?" The Bible teaches that your highest loyalty is to Jesus Christ. No parent has the right to command you to act in direct disobedience to God's Word. However, I've seen some young people who have twisted their Christian commitments into a clever rationalization for disobeying their parents. Granted, there are some bad parents who treat their children poorly. However, my observation has been that some of the worst parents, whose own lives are terribly mixed up, still have pretty good insights into their children. Some parents take better moral and spiritual care of their children than they take of themselves. Your parents have given you life, and never will you understand the enormous concern they have for you, even though they may be morally weak, until you have your own children. Obey your parents. Your chances of going wrong will be much slimmer than if you strike off on your own, rebelling against their authority.

Second, we are to respect our parents. This doesn't mean we have to agree with them on everything. Just plain human courtesy is something we're inclined to offer the rest of the world but fail to give our loved ones. It has been said that "obedience is temporary—respect is permanent!" It's difficult to respect a person when he or she is wrong. Yet with the very position of parenthood goes some degree of respect. It works the other way. Parents don't love only a lovable child. The very family bonds are good enough reason for respect and love. A society is destroyed when those family bonds are broken. Sad is a young person who has been disrespectful of his parents and only later, when they are gone, is able to realize the investment they've made.

Part of respecting one's parents is our willingness to listen to their counsel. The Bible says, "The fear of the Lord is the beginning of knowledge: fools despise wisdom and instruction. Hear, my son, your father's instruction, and reject not your mother's teaching; for they are a fair garland for your head, and pendants for your neck" (Prov. 1:7-9).

The sign of immaturity is apparent when the teenager strikes off on his own, making decisions spiritual, vocational, and romantic without the counsel of his parents. When a young person shares inner burdens of the heart with father and mother, listening to their advice, the sign of maturity is equally apparent.

I remember my dating days in high school, college, and

seminary. I remember bringing girls home for Mom and Dad to meet. Some were good-looking. Some were intelligent. Some were potentially good homemakers. Some were athletic. Some were spiritual. Some had excellent family backgrounds. Most of them combined a number of these traits, in varying degrees. I got serious with two or three. Mother and Father didn't warm up to any of them, but never were they unkind. In certain cases they thought the girl was wonderful. The only problem was that she was not for me. My parents knew me well. They had a better idea of what was good for me than did I.

It was amazing how, although I would get upset with the frankness with which my parents would answer my questions, ultimately their candid reactions proved to be correct, and eventually there would be a breakup of the romance. My parents could see these things more quickly than could I. On the other hand, I remember when I met Anne. I was traveling through the Far East. We had a brief encounter in Taipei, Formosa and again in Hong Kong. I fell deeply in love. There was only one problem. Anne was engaged to another young man and I had no assurance that she would ever be available or even remember me. I wrote my parents from Singapore thinking I would probably never see Anne again. They wrote back. The letter met me in New Delhi, India saying, "John, this time the girl seems right."

The story is too long to give all the details. Months later Anne came to a natural parting with her fiancé and our courtship began. My parents never met her until they flew from Chicago to Los Angeles for our engagement announcement party. When they met it was the meeting of old friends, for my parents had an inner sense of who was best for me. They were able to give me correct counsel even when they had not met the girl.

Anne's experience was the same with her parents. In that earlier engagement she had been planning marriage to a fine person, but that relationship didn't have her mother's blessing. Still, Anne could have gone ahead in an assertion of her own right and married whomever she wanted. In the final analysis, however, she listened to the counsel of her mother and avoided making what would have been a mistake.

This doesn't mean children and parents have to agree on everything. But as children, listen to the counsel of your parents and give their opinions a high priority in your decision-making. I'm not talking just about career and romance. Some of us who are well into the middle years are fortunate enough to still have living parents who can give counsel in many areas from their wealth of experience.

By now you're probably saying, "You're talking to kids. I'm an adult." We forget that this commandment speaks to children of all ages and too easily apply it only to youngsters who are still at home. Honor to parents involves a total life concern. The Bible says, "If any one does not provide for his relatives, and especially for his own family, he has disowned the faith and is worse than an unbeliever" (1 Tim. 5:8). The early church had widows just as we have today. Paul instructs children and grandchildren to take care of their parents and grandparents.

I think we upper-middle-class Americans are the worst violators of this command. Our stress is on youth, virility, activity. We tend to become irritated by the senile, the aged, the infirm. We resent anyone who ties us down, who lessens our mobility. Some of us cart our elders off to nursing homes not because they need the specialized care that only a nursing home can give, but because they provide a major inconvenience to our lifestyle. For a while we may live in guilt for our refusal to bear responsibility, but before long we begin to rationalize away our guilt, coming to a semblance of peace. Eventually our chickens may come home to roost. Our children know what's going on. They sense our lack of respect for our parents. And they are quick to bring the same dishonor to us.

I used to chair a hospital task force on aging. At our organizational meeting, we discussed our need to provide better care not only for the acutely ill but for those who have chronic illnesses that do not confine them to hospitals but do necessitate some continuing care. As we left, one of the doctors shared these words, "I'm amazed at how many families drop off their aging parents at the emergency room and drive away, leaving them all alone all day." What is there in us that causes us to dehumanize the elderly? What is there in us that causes us to pull back from providing care, no matter, how unpleasant, for those who once changed our diapers and cleaned up our vomit?

It's a joy to observe many who at great personal sacrifice are taking such good care of elderly parents. Some pay a real price for keeping them in their homes, or if they need the specialized care of nursing homes, are so faithful in their visitations.

Christ set an example. Not only did he obey his parents in his youth; one of his final words from the cross was to entrust the care of his mother into the hands of his most loving and faithful disciple, John.

There's more to honoring our parents than the provision of good physical care. We have a responsibility to be interested in them and to be interested in what interests them.

Through our parents and grandparents we have invaluable links with our family heritage. Too often we turn off the rambling discourse of an elderly parent, forgetting what lies within those words. Remember in Alex Haley's Roots Kizzy explaining to her son, Chicken George, why she couldn't marry her lover, Sam. With deep emotion she said, "Sam wasn't like us. Nobody ever told him where he come from. So he didn't have a dream of where he ought to be goin'."

Perhaps we ought to take a bit more time for the old-fashioned family reunion. It's time to encourage our children to spend more time with their grandparents and for us to reminisce at greater length with our own relatives. We need to sit down with the oldest living members of our families and let them talk and share with us the oral history that only they know.

This commandment differs from all the others. The other nine tell you what you cannot do, but this one has a promise. It reads, "Honor your father and your mother that your days may be long in the land which the Lord your God gives you." That's quite a promise. God says this is the way to live a quality life. Not only that: the promise works in reverse. Honor not your father and your mother and see what happens. D. L. Moody said, "I have lived over sixty years, and I have learned one thing if I have learned nothing else—that no man or woman who dishonors father or mother ever prospers." Religion that doesn't begin at home doesn't begin.

# 7.

# WHO, ME—KILL?

MURDER is news whether it be the murder of an un-known or a popular hero. The very word *Murder* catches our attention. The Bible speaks about it in its most crisp state-ment: "You shall not kill" (Exod. 20:13).

"Who, me—kill?" Yes! You and I both are murderers. No, you would never premeditatedly snuff out a human life. That's one definition of murder. There are, however, additional kill-ings which in much more subtle ways accomplish similar ends.

You and I commit murder when we use other persons for what we can get out of them—without thinking about their sanctity as persons. The average person wouldn't call this murder. But read your Bible carefully. Take a look at the biblical understanding of human life.

The Bible pictures the human being as created by God, a unique being with a soul and an eternal nature. This is what distinguishes him from animals. All life has a sanctity. The Bible forbids all that endangers life. We are to preserve it, prolong it, and do all we can to maximize its creative potential. Created in God's image, human life is special, and you and I are called to treat it with reverence.

The whole thrust of the Scriptures is a call to our humanization. Anything that dehumanizes you or me as persons is murder. Anything I do to exploit another person for my own selfish ends is to dehumanize—to murder—that other person. Those of us who would sit up most startled when addressed as murderers would slide down in our seats quite quickly when we stop to look at our lives and see the ways in which we daily rob other people of their humanity.

Several years ago the Jewish theologian Martin Buber died. One of his most significant contributions was his book *I and Thou.* Buber developed the thesis that there is a distinct difference between a person and a material object. What he was saying is that the organist who plays the organ so beautifully on Sunday mornings is different from the organ. The organist is a person. The organ is an object. The organ cannot play the organist. It cannot use him for its own purposes. It comes to life only as human talent brings to it musical expression. The minute the organist withdraws his fingers from the keyboard and lifts his feet from the pedals, the organ is silent.

Now, Buber is saying what the Bible constantly stresses: Not only is a person different from a material object; persons often use other persons as if they were material objects. This is how we dehumanize people. This is how we murder. It's one thing for me to stand in the pulpit on Sunday morning and strike it. There's no person to hurt. It's quite another thing for me to strike my wife or knock her around as if she were an object. It's one thing for me to push my car beyond the limits of its capability but quite another to push my secretary to the breaking point.

There are various types of murder. There's physical murder in which we literally take the life of another person in an unauthorized violent killing. This commandment speaks clearly to this point.

But there's also spiritual murder in which we do not treat other persons seriously enough. We show too little consideration of their strengths and weaknesses. We murder a person's good name by destroying it in casual conversation. We destroy persons by our bad example or kill by the temptations we put in their way. We ministers starve people to death when we compromise the Word of God to the point that it loses the substance of spiritual nourishment. We destroy when we lack the spiritual zeal to share the claims of Christ with men and women who are lost for eternity because we have not brought them the Good News of salvation.

God is the only one who knows right now whether we qualify for his salvation. Our attendance at church, our reading of religious books, our best efforts do not save us. As a pastor, I'm shocked when I'm told of persons who have been members of a congregation for years but have never received Jesus Christ as Savior. So often we preach with the presupposition that we're simply bringing nurture to the believer and forget that there may be persons here who are spiritually dead. If we do not preach the gospel, if we do not share the Good News, we are accomplices in spiritual murder. If we are unwilling to speak a word for Jesus Christ, we are spiritually murdering someone else. We are not offering that help which through the Holy Spirit's power can bring life eternal in Jesus Christ.

Picture a nurse assigned to a terminally ill patient. Her charge is dying of cancer. That nurse happens to have in her purse a vial filled with a cancer-curing medicine. Instead of sharing this life-giving liquid, this nurse ministers graciously to the dying patient—making her comfortable, checking her temperature, and injecting painkilling substances. Any sane person would consider this nurse a diabolical sadist, no matter how pleasant she appears. No one has the right to withhold healing, yet you and I do it daily. We work with persons who are terminally ill with sin. We know the way to salvation. Instead we smile, act nice, and hold that healing to ourselves.

Then there's psychological murder. Some of us who would never lift a hand against another person can, by our attitudes, destroy them. There's that hostility which lurks underneath the surface. That bitterness of a wife aimed at a husband, of a husband aimed at a wife. Hateful, hurtful attitudes covered by slick words so the children will not recognize them.

Whom are you dehumanizing? Destroying? Murdering? Is it your wife, who to you is no longer a person? Everyone else's wife may still maintain her personhood while the woman who sits beside you has become a thing. Perhaps it's your husband. No longer do you delight in him. You are taking him for granted. Perhaps it's your child, your business associate, or your neighbor. We can broaden the circle until every one of us sees individuals being dehumanized by our lack of sensitivity to their sanctity, to the personhood given them by God. Christ said that to hate someone is to murder him. How quick we are to kill.

Not only do we commit murder when we use another person. We also commit murder when we don't take good care of ourselves. How seldom we think of it in these terms.

Granted, we do think of suicide. That's direct self-murder. Many of us are horrified by the thought. If we're honest we'll admit that there are fleeting moments—for some, not so fleeting—when we ponder that potential escape from life's problems. Occasionally emotional sickness strikes. We despair of life, yearning to be released from our limitations. The command not to kill has literal, direct implications for the taking of one's own life. Suicide is not an option.

But, again, for most of us this is not a real temptation. We're inclined to be more guilty of an indirect suicide by failing to live responsibly or to take good care of the life which God has given us. Forgetting that we have a duty to preserve ourselves, some of us expose ourselves to unnecessary danger living lives as daredevils. Remember the movie *Grand Prix* which showed the behind-the-scenes life of a race driver. Occasionally one comes along who seems to be bent on self-destruction. Driving himself and his cars to their very limit, he seems to yearn subsconsciously to be destroyed. A more subtle indirect suicide is that of those who neglect the common ordinary means of preserving human life.

Are you taking care of your body? Are there certain physical problems for which you are not seeking available medical care? Smoking, drinking, gluttony are other methods of indirect suicide. "You shall not kill" applies to the use of your appetite, whether for food or beverage. Intemperance in any area destroys, dehumanizing us both physically and spiritually. What about your grief at the loss of a loved one? How empty is your life? That loss is real, but I know individuals who are strangling themselves with grief. They kill themselves in a gradual suicide while they mourn the loss of a loved one gone for a year or two.

Just as we commit murder when we don't take good care of our body, we commit a type of spiritual suicide when we neglect our spiritual life. Every few days I come in contact with individuals who make some sickly comment about their own neglect of God. It's amusing to see the various reactions people have to a minister. When I am introduced to a stranger simply as John Huffman, the conversation picks up as normal. When I'm introduced as the Reverend John Huffman, it's amazing how the conversation changes. Where the family tree sports a minister, the immediate response is "You know, my grandfather used to be a minister." Most likely, people who are not active in any church may comment about how they ought to start going to church again. Or one will casually remark, "We'll have to keep our language clean while we're around this preacher." I was once visiting in the home of some people I know. They had guests. The guests began musing about the fact that at one time they had been extremely active in their personal faith. They had been involved in the life of their home church. Then the family moved. They admitted that for over eight years they had not entered a church.

There's a gradual spiritual suicide that comes from the failure to stay alive and active in one's Christian faith. Spiritual atrophy can set in and harden your spiritual arteries. You neglect your prayer discipline. You fail to open your Bible.

Or perhaps you simply have never received Jesus Christ as Savior. You've heard a lot about him. You may have watched Billy Graham on television or perhaps you've heard other evangelistic preachers. At the same time you refuse to repent of sin and expose yourself to Christ's claims. Your failure to respond to God's love in Christ is the ultimate in committing spiritual suicide.

Where do you stand? You commit murder when you don't take good care of yourself, whether it be literal suicide, the neglect of your body, or spiritual self-destruction.

In discussing the command "You shall not kill," several ambiguous areas may already have come to your mind. We've noted that at its very heart this command is a call to avoid any kind of action which dehumanizes another or one's self. You know that it would be wrong to commit cold-blooded murder. It's unlikely that you would pull a gun on someone. But how far do we push this principle? What about self-defense? What about capital punishment? What about killing at war? What about abortion? What about euthanasia? These are extremely difficult questions. Fine Christians disagree as to how the Bible should be interpreted.

The Bible gives place to several types of killing. The death penalty was a frequent recourse ordained by God to assure the basic principle of this commandment—that mankind is not to be dehumanized. When killing is permitted or even commanded by the Bible, it is regarded as the consequence of a duty to preserve life in its very highest sense.

Take for an example self-defense. The Bible teaches that we have the right to defend ourselves. This is the only private situation in which to kill is correct. When we resist the one who is endeavoring to take our life, we are protecting the principle that everyone has the right to live. Arthur Sueltz tells about an old Quaker who once took the words "You shall not kill" literally. He lived his whole life as a strict pacifist. Then late one night, he heard the floorboards creak downstairs. Someone had broken in. Quietly he crept out of bed, grabbed his flashlight and hunting rifle, sneaked downstairs and came up behind the thief just as he made for the window. The old Quaker shouted, "Friend, I would not harm thee for the world, but thou art standing where I am about to shoot." [1]

There is a place for self-defense. However, the Bible does prohibit a private person from taking vengeance upon someone else who has already committed murder. Facing the possibility of death and therefore killing in self-defense is quite a different thing from engaging in a clan warfare that delivers personal vengeance, an eye for an eye and a tooth for a tooth. In each of us, as Jesus saw in his disciples, there seems to be a desire to have revenge. Remember that occasion when he walked into a Samaritan village and the people would not receive him. This made James and John angry. "Lord," they asked, knowing Christ's supernatural powers, "do you want us to bid fire come down from heaven and consume them?"

(Luke 9:54). But Jesus turned and rebuked them. Revenge is not a legitimate Christian motivation.

What about capital punishment? Is it legitimate? As a form of revenge, the Bible says no. But the Bible also says that capital punishment is reserved for the society in which a person lives. To kill in vengeance is to murder. For society carefully to carry out capital punishment in a sane, logical, orderly way is not murder. In fact, in certain situations it is justice, for, by refusing to allow men to take the lives of others into their own hands, it sets a high premium on life. Genesis 9:6 reads: "Whoever sheds the blood of man, by man shall his blood be shed; for God made man in his own image." Granted, this is a complicated issue. We should never take joy in capital punishment. Our motivation should never be vengeance, much as we may have that feeling momentarily in our heart for one who commits a heinous crime against society. Interestingly enough, God did not respond to the first murder with the use of capital punishment. When Cain killed Abel, God held him accountable, but he did not kill Cain. Instead he put a mark upon Cain which singled Cain out as a murderer. In essence, Cain lived his life in imprisonment of that fact, bearing that mark until the day he died.

The Bible warns against an individual's taking vengeance into his own hands. It makes a fascinating distinction between public and private vengeance. Any murderer could flee to certain refuge areas. There he was safe from the person who would normally take vengeance. He could stay in the city of refuge until it was ascertained by the leaders of the community whether his act of killing was an innocent mistake or an act of guile. If a man murdered without intent, he stayed in the sanctuary until the emotions cooled and it was safe to move back into society. If he was found to be guilty of murdering with intent, then he would be put to death by the community.

This is the difference between the hangman's noose of the Ku Klux Klan, which has private individuals taking justice into their own hands under the cloak of darkness, as compared to the hangman's noose resulting from the deliberations of a jury chosen at large from the community. The lack of capital punishment makes human life cheap. I see nothing in the Scripture that demands its abolishment. I see everything in the Scripture to protect the sanctity of human life. Human life cannot in my opinion be paid for by enforced confinement that lasts seven years or so and then leaves the murderer open to parole. Power over human life belongs primarily to God and is delegated to humans only through the duly authorized civil authorities. To eliminate capital punishment opens the door more and more to allow people to derive the kind of self-adulation and publicity recently achieved by some of our more notorious murderers and kidnappers. Although some Christian civil libertarians in all good faith decry the recent trends back to capital punishment and deny that it serves as a deterrent, I believe that a solid biblical case can be built for a careful, just trial leading to capital punishment for the duly convicted criminal.

What about war? War fits into a similar category. War, when embarked upon primarily to protect human life, is far easier to justify than war for the ends for which it often becomes twisted through "jingoism." Endeavoring to increase the nation's prestige, economy, territory, or military power is diabolical. Genuine endeavor to safeguard the liberty of countless thousands is right. Our involvement in activities which dehumanize the enemy, failing to see him as a helpless victim of a tragic conflict, is wrong. How quickly we can become engaged in ruthless thinking. To kill the enemy because of his atrocities, matching atrocity against atrocity, dehumanizes us and our enemy at the same time. The problem is that war is

not black and white. There are no easy, Christian answers to
some of these problems except to do all we can as individuals
to insure that our cause is just and our means to the end is a
righteous means.

Although I have deep appreciation for those who are called
to Christian pacifism, I believe there are times when we must
go to war. The same Jesus who instructs us to turn the other
cheek also demanded a reason from his tormenters as to why
they treated him the way they did. Jesus encountered military
men and touched their lives with physical and spiritual healing. He didn't tell them to change their profession, but he
brought about in them a changed motivation. I'm afraid that
we as a country are still wallowing in post-Vietnam guilt. We
made many mistakes. But I thank God that I don't live in
Cambodia. The Marxist alternative is not one to which we
are called to make a passive capitulation. If you lived in Nazi
Germany could you passively have allowed Hitler to destroy
six million Jews and dehumanize a nation? Is it a crime to
plot against Idi Amin when you can smell the rotting bodies on
that Kampala hillside?

And then there's abortion. This dilemma is one of the
toughest, isn't it? Which is more important, the life of the un-
born fetus or the life of the mother? When does life begin?
At conception? At the first heartbeat? At birth? What if there's
a strong suspicion of genetic defect? Many questions can be
raised. The Old Testament Law seemed to differentiate between a fetus and life outside of the womb. The person who
injured a woman, causing her to abort, had to pay a specific
penalty in money. Killing a walking, living person was a capital offense.

But granting all these many difficulties, we Christians must
never take abortion lightly as our Supreme Court has done in
opening the way for a married woman to procure an abortion

without her husband's consent and for a minor to kill her un-
born child without her parents' consent. This has made abortion the only surgical operation for which a minor does not
need parental permission. George F. Will, writing in *News-
week*, says, "It is neither surprising nor regrettable that the
abortion epidemic alarms many thoughtful people. Last year
there were a million legal abortions in the U.S. and 50 million
worldwide. The killing of fetuses on this scale is a revolution
against the judgment of generations."[2] Some use abortion as a
method of birth control. Now with amniocentesis, a needle
can be inserted into the womb to withdraw a small amount of
amniotic fluid surrounding the fetus. The physician can tell
whether a baby will be a boy or a girl. If the child is the
"wrong" sex, parents can, and some do, choose to have an
abortion. Is this right? Is it moral to take the right to life from
a fetus arbitrarily when our society cannot yet define when
life begins?

Some social scientists suggest that we "harvest" the dead.
When an encephalogram shows a flat brain wave, technically
it confirms that the person is dead though the body may still
be living as evidenced by heartbeat. Whole wards could be
filled with bodies hooked up to life-sustaining machines providing kidneys, hearts, and other internal organs on call.

We can raise the question about euthanasia. Should we get
rid of the elderly useless, the genetically maimed, any others
who are a drag on society? Apart from a biblical understanding
of life's sanctity, society becomes wide open to diabolical
abuses.

All of these things must be seen in the dimension of Jesus
Christ. Nothing must be done in a spirit of ruthlessness, but
all to the glory of God and the ongoing fidelity of his creation.
The best way to carry out the command, "You shall not kill,"
is to see ourselves and our fellowmen as divine creatures made

in the image of God. We have been defaced by sin. We are rebellious people. Each of us is guilty of murder when it comes to dehumanizing God's creation, yet every single one of us is capable of being spiritually regenerated. Every single one of us is called to true humanity, which comes only through restored creation.

Let us ask God to sensitize us to a greater respect for the sanctity of human life, to abide faithfully by the humanizing teachings of Scripture in regard to others and ourselves, and to pray for wisdom in those areas in which valid questions can be raised.

"You shall not commit adultery."
*Exodus* 20:14

# 8.
# THE SEXUAL "REVOLUTION"

EVERY TIME I mention sex from my pulpit, I get three or four complaints that the topic is inappropriate, that I should stick to the Bible and not deal with this somewhat sensational topic. Interestingly, those same messages stimulate many conversations, counseling appointments, and expressions of deep appreciation for frank grappling with real problems.

It is a responsibility of the pulpit to speak out on this issue. Why? Because God's authoritative Word has a lot to say about sex. God didn't hide his head in the sand. He gave us this creative potential and he has instructed us how it is best to be used.

In fact, God thought that this topic was important enough that he devoted one entire commandment to it and implicitly included it in at least three of the others. God said, "You shall not commit adultery" (Exod. 20:14). On other occasions, we'll address various aspects of this topic such as homosexuality and fornication, but in this chapter we'll deal specifically with adultery.

Webster's dictionary defines adultery as "voluntary sexual intercourse between a married man and someone other than his wife, or between a married woman and someone other than her husband."

Many articles currently being written stress that our sanctions against adultery are being revised to the point that in a few years from now such conversation will no longer be relevant. Soon every single aspect of the reproductive process can be controlled by "bio-engineering." The day has already come when the embryo and fetus can be developed *in vitro*, a test-tube situation in which normal mating between husband and wife is not needed. An egg can be fertilized in a laboratory. Sex and personal characteristics can be selected from a "gene bank," enabling the whole process of conception through birth to happen totally apart from the usual reproductive cycle. One observer questions:

> With old fears replaced by new freedoms, do the foundations of fidelity become an outmoded concept? And if sex outside the marriage bed is o.k., what happens to marriage itself? Do we marry for love, companionship, security? Are these lasting? Should we be prepared to change partners whenever there is a feeling on the part of either one that it's time for a change? Are the legal bonds of marriage nonsense? Is the ideal to be a purely personal arrangement without law or ceremony, a companionate arrangement such as those that are becoming increasingly common among college students?[1]

Questions such as these demand answers. But while these questions are being raised by reputable individuals, many other persons are plunging on, as men and women have done through all human history, practicing marital infidelity. Remember when Jane Fonda was married to Roger Vadim? I remember how startled I was by some things she said in an interview. She was telling about how much she loved her husband. Parenthetically she said, "I've been thinking about getting a divorce." The journalist fumbled for the correct words. She interrupted, "Maybe a divorce would be good for our relationship. Of course, we'd go on living together." She then told how she wanted one more baby, preferably by Vadim. But she added that there were several of her husband's friends with whom she would like to have babies, if pregnancy weren't so slow and the idea somewhat impractical. Fonda and Vadim have long since separated, but these morally incoherent comments reflect an attitude among a growing number of our society.

There are persons who are living in the carefree world of occasional infidelities. In clear contrast to all the relativities that emerge with academic advances in bio-engineering and the historic pattern of unfaithfulness in marriage, is the Word of God. It speaks with clarity, saying simply, "You shall not commit adultery." God's Word for today is just that straightforward and absolute. C. S. Lewis, in *Mere Christianity*, commented, "We grow up surrounded by propaganda in favor of unchastity. There are people who want to keep our sex instinct inflamed in order to make money out of us. Because, of course, a man with an obsession is a man who has very little sales resistance." [2] All one has to do is take a simple stroll past a news stand to see the truth of his words.

You know the many excuses which are given for adultery. Probably the most common is that love is no longer there. Granted, one of the most difficult situations I've had to face as a pastor is to counsel couples who, as teenagers, have plunged into marriage against the advice of parents and friends. They thought they loved each other. They began a family only to wake up a few years later with the realization that they had made a mistake. Now here they are involved in a marriage that they've kept together for the sake of children. There's no love. One or both are involved in an extramarital affair, rationalizing that there is no real love between husband and wife, and that there is authentic love with the third party.

Another excuse I hear quite commonly is, "Why should I be denied sex just because my partner is physically or mentally disabled?" There are tragic cases of physical disability and mental illness which do change the circumstances of a marriage. Some claim this as an excuse for unfaithfulness. Is it really?

Then unfaithfulness itself is often given as an excuse. "Why should I remain faithful to my partner who is running around with somebody else? If he (or she) can do it, I can, too. What's good for the goose is good for the gander."

Occasionally I come across the individual who doesn't even try to give an excuse. He's just doing what he wants to do. And he couldn't care less.

I pity these persons. They're only trying to find a rationalization to get around God's command. When God says, "You shall not commit adultery," he's offering the basis for the healthiest marital life possible. It's not meant to limit our activity. It's meant to free us from a life motivated by raw, animal impulses. We are persons. The very image of God is stamped into our being. We can make moral choices. God has entrusted to us the privilege of living responsibly. We are more than animals. We can live in a context that is healthy, creative; one that is the most productive for our own welfare, the welfare of our partner and the ultimate welfare of the children that are born to the relationship, and the society in which we live.

God has given us some options. Let's take a look at several of them.

Option one: We have the privilege of living in obedience or disobedience to God's will. God ordained marriage. It is built on fidelity. Marriage is two becoming one—not just in body, but in soul. God created male and female to be incomplete alone. There is fulfillment in coming together in a responsible relationship. God says, "Therefore a man leaves his father and his mother and cleaves to his wife, and they become one flesh. And the man and his wife were both naked, and were not ashamed" (Gen. 2:24–25).

The sexual relationship, the total blending of body and soul, was created by God to be beautiful. He created it for procreation, yes, but he created it also for recreation. Through it he enables a man and a woman to find joy in each other's person. It's not something designed only to reproduce the human race, a mechanical process which we somehow may think we must view as a little bit dirty. It's something good in and of itself. Nowhere in the Word of God do we see anything but the highest, exalted view of sex. It's not just an obligation of a wife to put up with a man's passion. It's the privilege of both husband and wife to find the physical and spiritual fulfillment in an expression of a most intimate relationship exclusive to them alone.

The very God who created sexuality has set down guidelines for how it functions best. Those guidelines include fidelity. Even when he allowed polygamy, there were responsibilities that went with the relationship, fidelities that had to be maintained. Adultery was a capital offense. Our first option, then, is either to live according to God's Word in obedience, or to disobey. In disobedience, we'll have to face whatever personal, psychological, social, or spiritual penalties we've created for ourselves.

Option two: We can approach marriage with a commitment

either to permanence or impermanence. Many young people, afraid of marriage, settle into common-law relationships. Not all sacrifice their ideals. They've seen too many marriages protected only by a fragile piece of paper that seems to have very little significance. Most of us still enter into marriage. But many who do have not settled, once and for all, the fact of its permanence. Granted, the vows are articulated at the ceremony. The contract is signed. The covenant has been negotiated. I wonder how many really stop to think about the significance of those vows.

When is the last time you pondered your marriage vows? Every so often it's good to hear them repeated. Talk about a total commitment, pledged with one's honor. They go something like this: "I take thee to be my wedded spouse; And I do promise and covenant; Before God and these witnesses; To be thy loving and faithful spouse; In plenty and in want; In joy and in sorrow; In sickness and in health; As long as we both shall live." Can anything be more complete? List all the excuses you can for marital infidelity and stack them up against these vows you took. There's no room for adultery, is there? There is no circumstance which gives you a way out of those vows. A marriage relationship is one of permanence—till death doth part. That's why the biblical penalty for adultery is death. Adultery is one of the most heinous activities of dishonesty in which a person can engage.

This approach runs so contrary to contemporary thinking. I talk with many young people who are scared to death that they'll make a mistake; who have cravings for instant gratification; who want everything right away without risk or investment. Permanence involves risk. It demands that we build the relationship. It requires that we expose ourselves to the potential hurt that one person can bring upon another. A life-long commitment does make you vulnerable. You're exposing yourself to another person who can potentially destroy you by his strengths and debilitate you by his weaknesses.

Not only does it have risks. It also runs contrary to our love for novelty. As our society becomes more and more hedonistic, we develop a lower tolerance for repetition, for patterns, for sameness. We are "neophiles," lovers of the new. This works against permanence. It minimizes one's commitment to being trustworthy. The result? Marriages which are really engagements, engagement being defined as that period of tentative commitment which will soon be exchanged for a permanent relationship. If you're not committed to permanence, you're not really free. You're not free to be yourself. You have to play a game. You have to put on a front. You have to make yourself as appealing as possible to your partner. But there's always that inner nagging fear that the least sign of weakness or the first mistake will bring rejection. So, far from being liberating, the option for impermanence leaves you on pins and needles.

Option three: We have a choice between stability or instability. Extramarital relations imply fickleness. The novelty of adultery wears thin. Though it seems to promise fulfillment and the secrecy of it brings momentary excitement, as the old saying goes, "Lust's practice is to make a joyful entrance, but she leaves in misery." This life is not stable. It's built upon unfaithfulness. You wouldn't consider breaking a business contract, yet there's no security for the extramarital relationship. A person who could engage in activities which repudiate vows once taken, no matter how slick his conversation is at the time, can once again repudiate his new vows of love and faithfulness. This fickleness is habit-forming, becoming a life pattern that is anything but happiness-producing.

Talk with pastors, psychologists, or psychiatrists who do

much marital counseling. Seldom do you find a happy adulterer. The problems compound. The initial excitement wears off. Peter A. Bertocci in his *Christian Century* article titled "Keeping Quality in Sexual Experience" says,

> . . . sexual experience has a way of running down when two persons are united at the pelvis only. Somehow that union is not enough; a new vacuum is created. Perhaps by finding a different body, a new technique, one can fill the void for a while. But does this search for variety, which can become no more than a process of sampling, give a person quality? [3]

Michael Novak states it in a slightly different way:

> The new sexual freedom has found an ironic way both to trivialize sex and to make it oppressive. The trivialization comes from taking the sense of the sacred out of sex, and reducing sex to the familiarity of a handshake or a diplomatic kiss.
>
> The oppression comes from forcing one's instincts and heart to be as "liberated" as one's head—from shaming one into guilt feelings for saying no, from insinuating fear about one's "hang-ups" or "Puritanism." Guilt is no less evident today than in former generations. Sexual torment is no less prevalent. They have merely changed their psychic habitat and form. [4]

Option four: We have a choice between that which is constructive or that which is destructive. Infidelity brings destruction. No longer can the adulterer trust himself (herself) and his (her) word. Personal relationship with God is harmed. Reputation suffers, for when the adulterer's activities become public knowledge, people will not forget. Proverbs states it so well, "He who commits adultery has no sense; he who does it destroys himself. Wounds and dishonor will he get, and his disgrace will not be wiped away" (Prov. 6:32–33).

The adulterer destroys his (her) spouse. No matter what the weaknesses that tend to drive a man or a woman to infidelity, each spouse has needs as a person and should not be discarded. Infidelity destroys families. Husbands and wives must be exclusively loyal to each other if we are to have strong families. Unfaithfulness is a costly business. Two who have become one are cut apart, destroying themselves and bringing instability and disharmony to the family. Puzzled children have to pick up the fragments of broken relationships and try to fit their lives back together in some meaningful pattern. This has to be done without the unity of a father and a mother who love each other in the beauty of what marriage was meant to be.

Infidelity also destroys society. Every man does what he feels like doing. Total anarchy takes over. No one is safe. No one is secure.

Faithfulness is essential. There's a good basis for fidelity in marriage.

You know, adultery is terribly subtle. I have several friends who have become entangled in it. I've seen an interesting pattern which can stand as an illustration and warning. Let me paint a picture of what I've observed through several of these people. We'll call this hypothetical composite person Mr. X. During college, he dated around, then settled on one girl. At graduation they married. Together they worked to put him through graduate school. They made sacrifices to get his education, and then applied themselves with diligence to the establishment of his career. Things appeared to be going well in the marriage relationship during those early years. Of course, there were the normal ups and downs that every marriage has. Yet overall it seemed to be a pretty good marriage.

As Mr. X became more successful, he began to realize that material objects were not providing everything he thought they would. He was bored. As any typical red-blooded man would, he enjoyed seeing an attractive girl walk by. One day as he was interviewing girls for the secretarial pool, one interviewee attracted his attention. He was aware that maybe she wasn't as good a secretary as some of the other applicants, but he was attracted to her. He went ahead and hired her on something other than her secretarial abilities.

For a few months he enjoyed having her around the office. Gradually, without his being totally aware of what was going on, the two of them began to spend more time together. The circumstances were innocent, but they went beyond the normal obligations of work. Their conversations became more intense. Finally, they verbalized their mutual attraction. For a while they resisted the temptation to get physically involved. But in the meantime, things at home were not quite as good as they used to be. Mr. X began to rationalize the situation. Finally, Mr. X gave in to a relationship that he originally would never have considered—a relationship he would not tolerate in those around him but a relationship of unfaithfulness in which he seemed to think he was doing what was right.

Our Mr. X is now a tragic figure, as were all those from whom I made up his composite picture. Several faces come to mind reminding me of sadness and pain. The most tragic result is the life distortion which comes to the broken relationships left in the wake of unfaithfulness. I've seen Mr. X try to extract himself from the web of events surrounding him, but finding the web holds him too closely in its clutches.

In some situations I've seen men literally hung-up on sex. They love their wife; but there's this third person who offers them sexual thrills. She doesn't have the reticence the man's wife has. And he forgets that the wife will do what the other girl won't. She makes the beds. She does the dishes. She typed his thesis. She went through birth pain several times. She's got more to do than be a sexual acrobat, though that's no excuse for her to forget his needs. At the same time, she is responsible to meet a much wider range of needs. And what's even sadder is to see Mr. X when he dissolves his marriage and finally marries this third person only to find that their relationship is no deeper than the physical attraction and they've married a whole new set of problems.

I have some very deep concerns about some of the Christian sex manuals now being published. On the positive side, it's great to see an honest discussion undergirded by the fact that God created sex and sex is good. Anyone who objects to this type of conversation from the pulpit because of what reaction our children might have is avoiding the fact that they're being sold a bill of goods day in and day out in the media. However, some of the more recent literature encourages a dehumanizing exploitation within the bonds of marriage. A woman is encouraged to entertain her husband sexually with the thought that he will then purchase her some material object. There can be a mutual manipulation of each other which actually is a subtle form of prostitution. Sex is only one part of marriage. It's a symbolic expression of a totality of intimacy. It's not an end in itself.

How does a Christian cope with the temptations to adultery?

He or she can flee associations that might lead to unfaithfulness. Anything that is a mild flirtation now but could lead to something far more serious can be cut off. When another person flirts sexually with you, or you allow your thoughts to go toward someone other than your partner, you are lessening the quality of your relationship. You are producing a substitute. Jesus put it on the line when he said, "You have heard that it was said, 'You shall not commit adultery.' But I say to you that every one who looks at a woman lustfully has already committed adultery with her in his heart" (Matt. 5:27–28).

Our President may have made a serious mistake in granting

an interview to *Playboy* magazine, but the content of that interview is as straightforward and understanding of God's position on our humanity as you'll find anywhere. Unfaithfulness begins in the mind. These mild flirtations are like a narcotic. A few innocent experiments expand into a world of addiction. The Old Testament picture is so graphic. There's Joseph in the house of Potiphar encountering a woman with immoral designs on him. Ultimately, Joseph had to run out of the house, fleeing the temptation. He lost his job and went to jail. Joseph bit the bullet. He kept himself clean and usable in God's service.

For those who may be caught up in this kind of thing where it's past the fairly innocent stage, there's the exciting possibility of God's forgiveness. I know that there are some adulterers present in my congregation from time to time. I know because I've been alerted by a couple of wives who have called me and told me that when their husbands are in our city on business over a weekend, they actually attend this church with their girlfriends. Listen. God's forgiveness doesn't say, "Go on in a relationship that is wrong—I've forgiven you." It says, "Be sorry for what you are doing. Ask my forgiveness. Repent. Change your ways. Cut off the relationship and I will forgive you and make you a whole person."

The fact that your own marriage may be in trouble isn't going to guarantee that there'll be a brand new beautiful love; for unfaithfulness has harmed the relationship. But there will be newness of life in knowing that God has forgiven you. If there's a genuine repentance, you'll be amazed at the result. If you are truly sorry for your unfaithfulness, the one you've wronged in this world may be more ready than you'd think to accept you back. Claim the love of Christ where human love has failed. Claim the forgiveness which God will give to you, but be a new person with an integrity in your marriage relationship.

A group of male chauvinists gathered around Jesus discussing theological matters. A commotion ensued. A woman caught in adultery was dragged into their midst and thrown on the ground in front of Jesus. The men waited to hear his judgment. Jesus stooped down, pretending not to hear them. They pestered him for his word, demanding that she should be stoned. Jesus lifted his face and said, "Let him who is without sin among you be the first to throw a stone at her" (John 8:7). Then he stooped down once again. Convicted by their own consciences, the men disappeared, every single one of them. Jesus was left alone with the woman. He said, "Woman, where are they? Has no one condemned you?" She said, "No one, Lord." And Jesus said, "Neither do I condemn you; go, and do not sin again" (John 8:10–11).

The message is clear. Jesus called her activities sin. With no equivocation, he challenged her to a new life. But first He offered her forgiveness before he set her free to a different lifestyle.

A sex sin is not the worst sin. Failure to receive Christ's forgiveness is. The Savior who died for your sin and mine, who rose triumphant from the dead, offers forgiveness for unfaithfulness and offers a challenge to a new life, impossible in your strength. Will you receive it?

# 9.
# HOW TO SWINDLE YOURSELF

THE BIBLE says, "You shall not steal." According to the Hebrew understanding of the word *steal*, this means that you and I are not to take by stealth, secrecy, or force that which belongs to another.

This immediately raises a question. What is meant by belonging to someone? This commandment implies that we have the right to ownership. We are entitled to private property. God has given us the privilege of owning personal possessions.

Ownership is our right. Our minds think immediately of material things. We have a right to these. This also involves such possessions as reputation, health, and the spirit of wellbeing. When God created Adam and Eve, the Scriptures record:

And God blessed them, and God said to them, "Be fruitful and multiply, and fill the earth and subdue it; and have dominion over the fish of the sea and over the birds of the air and over every living thing that moves upon the earth." And God said, "Behold, I have given you every plant yielding seed which is

106

upon the face of all the earth, and every tree with seed in its fruit; you shall have them for food. And to every beast of the earth, and to every bird of the air, and to everything that creeps on the earth, everything that has the breath of life, I have given every green plant for food" . . . (Gen. 1:28–30).

This is God's order. You and I are to be in charge of his creation. We are responsible for that part of it which we personally own.

This is not the whole story, though some would stop at this point and use this text to underline the divine right of private property. They would forget to go on and point out that we are responsible not only for that part which we personally own, but we are also to have a concern for the ultimate well-being of all God's creation. We share a mutual concern with others. The God who has created us in his image speaks out in justice against any distortion of his creation. He has an ecological concern. We are not to rape and plunder each other, stealing from another that which is rightfully his. Nor are we to deface this creation over which God has given us stewardship.

In any discussion about private property, you and I need to realize that there is a much deeper underlying principle. It's best articulated in Psalm 24:1: "The earth is the Lord's and the fulness thereof, the world and those who dwell therein."

Our very right to exist comes from him. Every possession you and I have is a gift of God. Instead of clutching on so tightly, we might better see ourselves as stewards who have the privilege of maintenance. We're to do the best with what God has given us. We are not to latch on greedily. Ours is to be that generous spirit of a steward who has a trustee relationship to take care of someone else's possessions.

Immediately the problem of community ownership comes to mind. Not everything is private property. Through communal ownership we share together public property. Some use the

Genesis account to speak out against public education, public utilities, and the various services provided by local, state, and federal government. All of us complain about taxes. So that our needs will be better served, the Scriptures do not forbid either taxation or community ownership of certain properties. The principle we see coming into focus is that of a voluntary standing-together of individuals created in the image of God who will work together to accomplish certain desired ends. Therefore, we pool some of our private assets into what we call society. This way we're enabled to get along better.

Imagine what it would be like if each one of us owned our own postal system. As you figure up your taxes and complain about them, pause to think what it would be like if our roads were private. You and I would be subject to extortionate toll rates if we wanted to use someone else's road. Community ownership is permissible, but only on a voluntary basis.

If you don't like the rules of the city in which you live, work to change them. Or, you have the privilege of moving to another city which has rules you like better. Citizenship in a free country is sort of like belonging to a club. You don't have to pay the dues, but if you don't, you are no longer entitled to receive the benefits of the club. A person who does not agree with the laws of the land in which he lives is entitled to move to another country. If he stays, he must be subject to those laws and carry his responsibility in the servicing of the community needs.

It's at this point that Marxism differs from the community ownership that you and I know in our Western lifestyle. Dialectical materialism strips private property from individual men and women and gives this ownership to the government. Communism is based on dictatorial powers. Marx called it the "dictatorship of the proletariat" in which private property and wealth of various types are taken from the ruling class by a violent social overthrow of the existing structure. A new god is substituted. This god is called the State. The State becomes a substitute for the God of Abraham, Isaac, and Jacob, the God who has revealed himself in Jesus Christ, creating you and me as human beings to have dominion over the earth. Communism is not the only "ism" that has made this substitute. At the other extreme, fascism is equally dictatorial. Once again the State becomes supreme. It owns the means of production. The individual person created in the image of God becomes increasingly insignificant.

For us to be the persons we were created to be, we must be guaranteed the right of ownership. We have the right to our own bodies. We have a right to our own souls. We have the right to our own material possessions. You and I are created in the image of God with the capacity to choose. Ultimately we are responsible only to Jesus Christ for the way in which we live our lives and handle our possessions. Societally or individually, any variation from the code of God which says "You shall not steal" will lead to the destruction of society and in turn, of ourselves.

Up to this point our conversation has been somewhat abstract. Let's get a bit more practical. Commandment Eight says, "You shall not steal." We're not thieves, are we? It's a good commandment to have on the books. It keeps society under control. There are laws to protect us from the thief. So we might as well close the book and consider the lesson complete, right? Stop a moment. Let's look at ourselves under the microscope of God's Word. When we do this we see that stealing is more common than we think. Both you and I are implicated. Nothing is easier than for us to rationalize our way around the command, "You shall not." There are various ways in which we carry out our subtle swindle. We do it against others, against ourselves, and against our God. A close mirroring of our activities would picture a profile on "How to Swindle Yourself," for our subtle thefts against others and our God ultimately become larceny against ourselves. We end up paying the price.

First, we swindle ourselves by stealing from others.

Stealing from others can be an outside job. There's the ordinary thief who breaks into a home. There is the usurer, the person who lends money at an exorbitant fee. You've read about loan sharks who grab hold of their helpless victims and drain their financial life-blood. Unfortunately, there are Christian loan sharks who have never tied their business ethics to their own personal relationship to Christ. There are other outside jobs. There is the playing of legal tricks in which one reads the fine print of which someone else is unaware, and in the process makes an extra buck off him. There is the borrower who never intends to repay. Or, the person who knowingly receives stolen goods from a black market operation is this kind of a thief. The merchant who puts his thumb on the meat scale of his business, hiking prices in a way which leaves the helpless purchaser with no recourse; this man, too, is a thief. A vandal is a robber. Teenagers on a late evening joyride, cutting corners over a lawn, are robbing someone of their time, energy, and money. Or it can be cheating on examinations. By putting down an answer that belongs to someone else you're detracting from his rightly earned academic standing and parading under a grade that is not justly yours. Something as simple as littering our streets steals from the beauty of God's creation. These are all outside jobs.

Then there's the inside job. This is much more subtle. We pull off an inside job when we rob our employer by not giving a good day's work. Or we pad our expense account. (That hits home, doesn't it?) We can rationalize this one by saying, "I am more worthy than the pay I'm getting; what would this company do without me?" So we give ourselves a little indirect pay raise by exaggerating our expenses or by stealing supplies from

the office. Bishop Alfred Stanway told the story of a man em-
ployed by a supply company who built a new home. Many of
the supplies he stole from his company. This man would never
have thought of pulling a truck up to a department store ware-
house and hijacking a load of furniture. But isn't that precisely
what he did? What you have around your home that belongs to
the business which employs you, that you're not using to carry
out your work, is not yours but something stolen. Your failure
and mine to do the best job we can is an inside job of hijacking.
The trustee of another person's funds who has taken on the
responsibility of helping that other person is guilty if he is making poor use of those funds. This is the inside job.

Stealing from others has a broader meaning than we usually
give it. It's not only the vice of the have-not who rips off the one
who has. It works the other way also. Too often this command
not to steal is used as a shelter for wealth which abuses. This
commandment calls to industry. But it does not call to the exploitation of others. When we think of a thief, we almost always
immediately think of a poor man, underprivileged, as the one
who breaks in and steals. But the rich can steal as well as the
poor. The rich man robs the poor when he doesn't use his riches
for the advancement of the Kingdom of God and the betterment
of his fellowman. You and I rob society when we take from it
and don't put back into it. There's a subtle danger of using
this commandment. There's an ultra-selfish rationalization for
tightly holding onto wealth in a refusal to help others. Reading
a Charles Dickens novel, we are amazed that little children
could be forced to work twelve, fifteen, eighteen hours in the
sweatshops of old England while the industrialists got rich off
this child labor. At the same time, some of us employers squeeze
the last bit of work out of our employees for the very least
amount of money we can give them. There are housewives who
resent the maid who hints that she needs a raise for that one

day's work. Sixteen dollars seems like an awful lot. Now she wants eighteen or twenty. And that maid observes her employer spend half, or perhaps even all that amount at the beauty parlor, while she supports herself and several children on that money. The same society that taxes also helps us make our fortune. The same private property which is inviolable must also be used to help other persons.

God has allowed some people to prosper materially. If you're one of these, your wealth doesn't mean that you are better than someone else. With that prosperity goes responsibility. Remember a few years ago the movie *The Unsinkable Molly Brown*. The main characters were a couple from the mountains of Colorado who had practically nothing of this world's goods. Suddenly they came into enormous wealth when they discovered a rich vein of minerals. Catapulted overnight into millionaire status, they traveled around the world trying to find happiness and friends. They threw lavish parties. They built enormous homes. They didn't work. They failed to realize that they owed a debt to the society that gave them access to their mine and value to their commodity. Wealth is not always an index of industry. The lack of wealth is not always an indicator that the poor man has not worked hard and shown human initiative.

This pride which some of us take in our productivity has produced the very communism which we fear. Communism is actually a Christian heresy. For a fascinating experience, take some time to read *Das Kapital* by Karl Marx. At certain points you'll begin to think that you're reading Christian theology. Why? Because Marx put his finger on a basic human flaw. He noted that when persons get into positions of power, they tend to exploit other persons.

Instead of developing his view of human nature along the revolutionary lines of the Scriptures, which call those of us who have to help those who have not, he called for a different revolution. He said the ruling class pays the working man a sub-sistence wage, giving him just enough to stay alive so he can put in another hard day at the factory. Then the ruling class takes the product, sells it at a profit, gets rich on the markup while the poor working man barely holds body and soul to-gether. What's the answer? The violent overthrow of the rulers by the proletariat, the working man. Then a new day will dawn.

Do you catch the eschatological note? It almost parallels the biblical promise that Christ will some day return. All wrongs will be set right. No wonder communism is so attractive to people all over the world who work so hard and have so little to show for it.

Don't misunderstand me; I am a capitalist. But I'm called to be a Christian first. A Christian is not a whole Christian whose heart is not touched by the needs of others who are willing to work. Skills should be adequately rewarded. Communism is a heresy. It makes a false promise. Show me a country in which communism has come to power where the average citizen has the freedom God intended for him to have. Yet it has enormous appeal. Its promises are great because of those of us who have not always shared the way we should. We have been robbers of the poor, not only in our own country, but abroad. We ulti-mately bring the revolution upon ourselves. Christ doesn't call us to change because we're afraid. He calls us to change be-cause it's right.

Arthur Sueltz tells a story about an old-time mayor of Toledo who earned the name "Golden Rule" Jones. Every so often he would go down and preside at the police court. On a winter day during the depression of the 1930s, the police brought in a man charged with stealing groceries. The man pleaded guilty; he offered no excuse except that he had no money and no job.

"I've got to fine you," said the mayor. "You stole, not from the community responsible for these conditions, but from a particular man. So I fine you $10.00."

But then the mayor reached into his pocket and pulled out a bill. He said, "Here's the money to pay your fine." Then he picked up his hat and handed it to the bailiff. "Now I'm going to fine everybody in this courtroom fifty cents, or as much thereof as he happens to have with him, for living in a town in which a man has to steal groceries in order to eat. Bailiff, go through the courtroom and collect the fines and give them to the defendant." [1]

The Bible makes it very clear that we have responsibilities to others. We're not to rob them by the outside job, the inside job, or by insensitive exploitation. The Bible says: "You shall not steal, nor deal falsely, nor lie to one another. And you shall not swear by my name falsely, and so profane the name of your God: I am the Lord. You shall not oppress your neighbor or rob him. The wages of a hired servant shall not remain with you all night until the morning" (Lev. 19:11–13).

Then there's that swindle of one's self, something that happens more commonly than we realize. The person who is stingy with himself and with his family robs himself and his family of so much that could contribute to meaningful life. Then for every niggardly person who hides everything away in a sock, there's a foolish spender who's stealing from himself as he makes no provision for the future. He's insensitive to the long-range needs of his family. Idleness—that lack of industry which does not respond to the responsibilities God has given you—is stealing. Some people work too hard robbing the joy from life and some people don't work hard enough, and thereby do not find the great joy that comes through being the person God created them to be.

Washington psychoanalyst Michael Maccoby has just writ-

ten a book titled *The Gamesman*.[2] He's made a study of the
various types of managers who make it at the top in well-run
corporations. He identifies four types. One is the "craftsman,"
the gentle holder of traditional values who is absorbed in his
own specialty. Another is the "jungle-fighter," the dog-eat-dog
type of person, who destroys his peers and superiors and ultimately himself. Another is the "company man" who is occasionally effective, but lacks the daring to bring about bold
changes. The real winner in business is "the gamesman." He
loves glory in winning, not necessarily for the sake of wealth
and power, but for the sheer joy of victory. He hates to lose.
Most successful executives combine several of these personali-
ties, but the "gamesman" in them seems to be the most domi-
nant strain. Maccoby discovered that there is a troublesome
aspect to this personality profile. For all his success and financial
reward, the "gamesman" admits that his work does little to
stimulate what Maccoby calls "the qualities of the heart," such
as loyalty, a sense of humor, friendliness, and compassion. They
may display those qualities at home, but the games executives
play do not encourage the heart to develop at the office.

There's a third swindle you can perpetrate on yourself. It's
stealing from God. Perhaps you're guilty of this theft. All you
have is his. "Every good and perfect gift comes from him." His
ownership is supreme. You've done your best to guard yourself
from the other abuses we've mentioned, but you've held back
from God that which is rightfully his. Perhaps you've held back
your talent. You have gifts which the community of believers
needs. There are things you can do that will complement the
Body of Christ. Your church needs you and your gifts and you
have protected yourself from getting involved. Perhaps you've
held back your love from the Lord. Yours is not a lifestyle of
adoration. Seldom do you truly worship. Perhaps you've held

back your tithe. Oh, you may give a few hundred dollars a year for Christ's work, but you're not tithing. You've got every rationalization in the world. Read what God has to say:

> "Will man rob God? Yet you are robbing me. But you say, 'How are we robbing thee?' In your tithes and offerings. You are cursed with a curse, for you are robbing me; the whole nation of you. Bring the full tithes into the storehouse, that there may be food in my house; and thereby put me to the test, says the Lord of hosts, if I will not open the windows of heaven for you and pour down for you an overflowing blessing" (Mal. 3:8–11).

Perhaps you're holding back your family. I'm reminded of a mother and a father who had committed their lives to Jesus Christ. They had only one child, who also became a Christian, and eventually sensed the call of God to go to the mission field. At this point, the father and mother held back on God, depriving him of what was rightfully his by doing everything they could to block their daughter from obeying God's call. We steal from God when we hold back total commitment of our lives to God, or even when we hold back some isolated portion of our lives while claiming to be real Christians.

By the time we look at these various ways in which we swindle others and in turn, ourselves, we realize that every one of us stands guilty. How subtle are the ways in which we violate others, ourselves, and God.

Doesn't it boil down to the fact that thievery of any type is, at heart, an expression of disbelief? Jesus Christ has promised to supply our needs according to his riches in glory. The very fact that we have grasping, clinging hands is reflective of the fact that there's a selfish urge in our lives which needs the transformation only Christ can bring. He calls us to give our lives to him in faith. He calls us to trust him to provide materially through the lean times. He calls us to understand that our possessions can be curses instead of blessings when these riches are not part of his will. He calls us never to embark on a course of action, pursuing material things which cannot claim his blessing. If even for a moment we doubt whether or not he favors a course of action we are taking—in regard to others, ourselves, or him—we'd better stop, wait, or readjust our course of action until we get the forward order from him.

Wherever you and I have failed, the Lord calls us to restitution. Remember Zacchaeus? Alerted to his crooked ways, he restored fourfold. Perhaps you and I need to make some restitution.

There's a positive note to all of this. A Christian who takes this commandment seriously will impress the world with the quality of his commitment. Several weeks ago, I picked up a tennis game with a vacationing motel owner from Urbana, Illinois. After a couple of sets, I asked him if any of the Inter-Varsity college students stayed at his motel during the big Urbana missionary conference in December. He said, "They take our whole motel over for each of their conventions. You know what? Those kids are the very finest. I usually calculate 12 percent additional cost into my motel rates to cover routine theft. I've never lost so much as one towel when those kids are in town."

You and I can't be perfect. But the world will quickly see if you and I are serious in our attempt to obey this command. What an opportunity is ours!

*"You shall not bear false witness against your neighbor."*
*Exodus 20:16*

# 10.
# LOOKING YOURSELF
# IN THE EYE

Newspaper columnist Sidney J. Harris published an article titled "Useful Phrases Interpreted." In his short dictionary of everyday phrases, Harris pointed out our tendency toward deception. His thesis was that our comments need to be decoded if we are to arrive at the truth. Here are some examples of how deceptive we are to others and to ourselves.

"Excuse me" means "Get out of my way!"

"Can I help you?" means "What are you doing here?"

"With all respect for your opinion" means "I have no respect for your opinion."

"The honest truth" means "The smallest lie I can tell you."

"Let's get together some time" means "Not if I see you coming."

"I didn't realize I was driving that fast" means "I didn't realize there was a squad car behind me."

"That is quite a spirited child you have there" means "You ought to put a leash and muzzle on him."

"You haven't changed in 20 years" means "Great heavens, was that senile creature in my high school class?"

"We have an early day tomorrow" means "Another half-hour here and we'll perish from boredom."

"Not that it's any of my business" means "I'm going to make it my business whether you like it or not."

"Don't breathe this to a soul" means "That's the same thing I was told, but I ignored it."

"The facts speak for themselves" means "Those facts I have carefully selected and arranged speak for what I want them to say."

"Every fair-minded citizen" means "Every citizen who shares my particular biases."

"Of course I hardly know her" means "This won't stop me from telling the worse of what I suspect."

"I'm looking for constructive criticism" means "Buck me up!"

Is it possible that you and I twist the truth in various ways just about every day? Sometimes we do it innocently. Other times we are purposefully devious. And there are various shades in between.

From earliest times, society has grappled with ways of enforcing truth. Ever since Adam and Eve rebelled against God, mankind has been plagued with a bent toward dishonesty. However, even secular society does its best to redirect this bent. Integrity is essential if there is to be a healthy functioning of human interaction. That's why we have codes of law.

Way back in Babylonian times, the secular law code of Hammurabi enforced a serious penalty upon the person who gave false witness in a law court. If the judge discovered the perjury, the man bearing false witness was to suffer from the crime of which he falsely accused another person. Perjury is serious business. In our own country, the accused Communist Alger Hiss was not sentenced for communism but for perjury. He went to jail for bearing false witness. Then we've seen what happened to the person who helped put him in jail. Years later, that man went on to be President of the United States. Now he lives discredited for his dishonesties.

If only you and I could master Commandment Nine, how much better off we'd be. "You shall not bear false witness against your neighbor." God knows our human tendency. He underlines without equivocation the seriousness of honor. Some people like to think that Jesus loosened up the Old Testament law. Wait a moment. Read his warning as to how you and I can become distorted.

> "You brood of vipers! How can you speak good, when you are evil? For out of the abundance of the heart the mouth speaks. The good man out of his good treasure brings forth good, and the evil man out of his evil treasure brings forth evil. I tell you, on the day of judgment men will render account for every careless word they utter; for by your words you will be justified, and by your words you will be condemned" (Matt. 12:34–37).

What a warning! On another occasion Jesus took a more positive approach. Underlining the importance of both spiritual and ethical truth, he says ". . . If you continue in my word, you are truly my disciples, and you will know the truth, and the truth will make you free" (John 8:31–32).

The Bible calls for honesty in all of our dealings with other persons. Our human associations are to be marked with integrity. This Ninth Commandment says that when we make a statement about another person, it must be true. And even those statements of fact must be made in a way that convey the correct impression. What I'm trying to say is that you and I can make true statements which convey falsehood. I could make the statement "John Doe's ethics are improving." It's a true statement. I know him to be a man who, with God's help, is endeavoring to live each day closer to the Lord. He strives continually to be a man of Christian integrity. I notice constant growth in spiritual maturity. But is that the impression I leave with my offhand comment? You have no way of knowing where he started out. Perhaps he's a person whose lifestyle has been marked by dishonesty and only recently has become more a man of his word. I could say that John Doe is treating his wife, Jane, much better these days. It's true. But you immediately wonder what awful kind of person he had been. He always did treat her well. The fact that he is simply growing in Christian grace can be eclipsed by the tone of voice or implication. You and I can do untold damage while maintaining technical truth.

This commandment is one of the easiest to break. That's why James wrote at such length about the tongue. He says:

> All of us often go wrong; the man who never says a wrong thing is a perfect character, able to bridle his whole being. If we put bits into horses' mouths to make them obey our will, we can direct their whole body. Or think of ships: large they may be, yet even when driven by strong gales they can be directed by a tiny rudder on whatever course the helmsman chooses. So with the tongue. It is a small member but it can make huge claims.
>
> What an immense stack of timber can be set ablaze by the tiniest spark! And the tongue is in effect a fire. It represents among our members the world with all its wickedness; it pollutes our whole being; it keeps the wheel of our existence red-hot, and its flames are fed by hell. Beasts and birds of every kind, creatures that crawl on the ground or swim in the sea, can be subdued and have been subdued by mankind; but no man can subdue the tongue. It is an intractable evil, charged with deadly venom. We use it to sing the praises of our Lord and Father, and we use it to invoke curses upon our fellowmen who are made in God's likeness. Out of the same mouth come praises and curses. My brothers, this should not be so (James 3:2–10, NEB).

Let's get specific. There's the subtle danger of gossip. This can destroy our personal relationships. The most precious possession we have is our reputation. How quickly our honor can be lost by a word of innuendo or a blatant piece of gossip. Perjury kills a man's reputation. Gossip so quickly becomes the assassination of character. The danger of second-person tale-bearing is that the story grows in the retelling.

One of my good friends, Wilton Maynard, used to share with me a phrase that is so appropriate when it comes to gossip. If you're tempted to hand out hearsay, he says, ask yourself, "Does my rumor have a sponsor? Where did I get the information? Am I willing to put my name on it as a sponsor?"

Think that one through. If you and I are going to tell a story about someone else, we are becoming its sponsor. We are testifying to its truth by who we are and by the fact that we're saying it. If it ultimately proves to be wrong, our own credibility is lessened. I'm learning that I have to think twice before I say something because, whether I like it or not, I become that rumor's sponsor.

This fact is well illustrated by a story from the life of Abraham Lincoln. Apparently the charge that Mr. Lincoln was an infidel was freely made during his campaign for Congress against Peter Cartwright, whom Lincoln defeated. Mr. Lincoln replied to the charge with a letter to the editor in which he said, "Mr. Woodward . . . may have believed what he said; but there is, even in that charitable view of his case, one lesson in morals which he might, not without profit, learn even of me—and that is, never to add the weight of his character to a charge against his fellowman, without knowing it to be true—I believe it is an established maxim in morals that he who makes an assertion without knowing whether it is true or false, is guilty of falsehood; and the accidental truth of the assertion, does not justify or excuse him." [1]

Then there's the not-so-subtle danger of slander. We'd best be careful if we call a man a liar to be certain we're right, or we ourselves become the liar. There's no protection against slander. No matter how good a life we lead, we are susceptible to this poisoned dart. Holiness, closeness to God does not fully exempt a person from being damaged by a vicious tongue. O that we could be constantly reminded to avoid whatever brings destruction to the character of another. How fortunate you are if slander has not been directed your way. It's important that you and I as Christians lend our every effort to smothering slander's fast-moving flames. If you are a victim, all you can do is trust God ultimately to vindicate you. Many men and women of God have found their testimony for Christ blunted by an accusation that has no foundation. Fortunately, "God's payday is not always Friday." He protects his own. But the potential damage is fearsome. We are to avoid anything that prejudices our neighbor.

Young people are especially sensitive to this. Some complain that the church is filled with hypocrites because of our tendency to jump to conclusions about other people. I think we're learning some lessons. We're discovering that just because a young person wears long hair doesn't mean that he's caught up in drug usage; just because he has short hair doesn't mean his life is clean. Some of us have learned these lessons the painful way. At the same time, young persons have to face the fact that just because we're puzzled by some fast-changing youthful practices doesn't necessarily mean we're making prejudiced judgments. Slander is a two-way street. We drive people away from our Lord when we as Christians participate in anything that destroys the one precious thing every person has, his honor.

There's no place for dishonesty of any type. Lying immediately brings with it other sins. Even as another man's name is one of the most valuable possessions he has, the integrity of your word is one of the most valuable possessions you have. Even if it hurts to maintain it, honesty is the best policy. This is equally true in family relationships, in business, and in social life. There's no place for a false witness even when it is a dishonesty that is geared to protect another person from hurt. Distorting the truth in an effort to build a shield around someone else doesn't work. So often the ricochet hurts another or even yourself. Jesus said, "Let what you say be simply 'Yes' or 'No'; anything more than this comes from evil" (Matt. 5:37).

This raises some real questions, doesn't it? You ask, "What about the truth that hurts? Am I supposed to say everything?" God's call is for you not to be brutal with the truth.

A lady shared this dilemma with me. Her next-door neighbor invited her over for coffee to see the neighbor's newly decorated home. No sooner had my friend stepped inside than she became almost sick at what she considered the poor taste in colors and furnishings. Needless to say, the next question was, "What do you think of it?" What should one do in a situation like that? Some people prefer the flattering lie to the unflattering truth. Sophocles, writing in the year 408 B.C., suggested, "Truly, to tell lies is not honorable, but when the truth entails tremendous ruin, to speak dishonorably is pardonable." Do you believe that? I'm afraid too many Christians do. Obviously there's a tension between telling the truth to someone else's hurt and being courteous to the point of dishonesty. Nowhere do the Scriptures say that we have to tell everything. But they do call us to tell the truth in love, being honest in a way which speaks productively to the betterment of the other person. Perhaps my friend could have discovered something she liked about the newly redecorated home. She could concentrate on the positive and minimize the negative without compromising her integrity.

Then there's the problem of rumor—those stories which, while making the rounds, become elaborated from mouth to mouth. Right now the makers of Bubble Yum are going crazy. Up until recently it was the most popular gum item to come along in the past ten years. Then two rumors got out—one, that the product causes cancer; another, that Bubble Yum has spider eggs in it. And many kids believe the rumors. To combat them, the Lifesaver Company which manufactures this bubble gum has hired private investigators to trace their origins. It has also placed full page ads in thirty newspapers in northern New Jersey, southern Connecticut, and New York proclaiming, "Someone Is Telling Your Kids Very Bad Lies About A Very Good Gum."

I'll never forget the rumor that spread like wildfire through Tulsa, Oklahoma, some ten years ago. The word got out that a workman at the local Pepsi-Cola bottling plant had disappeared several weeks before. Then the story spread that he had slid into one of the syrup vats and his decomposed body had just been discovered. Imagine what this baseless rumor did to sales.

D. L. Moody used to suggest that when someone fills your ear with a rumor, you offer to check out its truthfulness right away. It's amazing how many people will back off from it the moment you suggest verification.

The Bible also calls for honesty with ourselves. Take a look at your own lifestyle. Are you happy with your work? Are you happy with your friends? Is your marriage a productive marriage? There's nothing admirable about self-deception. It's foolish. Take the golfer who "fudges" on his score. I'm not referring to someone in a tournament whose score must be posted; I'm talking about the golfer who enjoys playing the game for his own fun. As he plays, he shifts the ball to better his lies. He forgets to count a stroke here and there. He takes two or three "mulligans" in the course of the game, ending up with a score that looks pretty good but is not an honest record of how he played. Ultimately this self-deception will catch up with him. The next time he plays he will either be discouraged by the correct score in relationship to the phony score of the time before or he will catch himself up in an ever-increasing cycle of self-deception. The game is only fun when we play it by the rules. We enjoy our successes only when we're honest about our failures. Failure which is called success is self-deception!

At times this self-deception can backfire. Once Anne and I went out to dinner with another couple. We got to talking about self-deception. The girl, Mary, told how it backfired on her. As a teenager one day in a Latin class, she was taking an exam. When she ran into a snag, she yielded to her weaker impulse to cheat. She borrowed some answers from the girl at the desk next to her. Much to Mary's surprise she found out that her cheating not only hurt others but herself. She had lifted the correct answers from her friend's paper thereby turning in such a good examination that unbeknownst to her, she won the honor of representing her high school in the statewide Latin contest. You should have heard her describe her mixed feelings of guilt and shock which she carried with her into the contest. She knew she had not qualified honestly and her miserable showing confirmed her inner feelings.

Be honest with yourself. Even if it demands something drastic in your life. Take whatever steps are necessary to rejuvenate your marriage. Bring new zest to your job. And increase the quality of your friendships. It may be time for you to have a new beginning. Some years ago, Anatoly Kuznetsov, the Russian writer, got up the courage to flee from his homeland. For years he had suffered literary suppression. He carried with him microfilm of his original manuscripts which had been censored and edited in their Soviet publication. His previous adaptations to censorship embarrassed him. After arriving in London, England, he met with a few friends and conducted a small memorial service for the dead, paying respects to the late author Comrade Kuznetsov and offering a toast to his successor, Mr. A. Anatole. He buried his previous life and name to start over anew in total honesty to his convictions as a writer. Real self-honesty, at times, demands a funeral and a new birth. Perhaps you need a dramatic change.

Nowhere is self-honesty more important than in your relationship with God. Jesus had disregard for those people who made verbal professions about their faith, but were phony inside. He said, "Why call me Lord, Lord, and do not the things which I command you?" Jesus calls you to be yourself. He doesn't want you to pattern after someone else.

I remember reading an article titled "I Am What I Am," by Mrs. Gary DeWitt.[2] She told of picking up a stunning piece of material and a designer pattern to go with it. She was so impressed with how the model looked on the cover of the pattern. She worked hard making the dress only to be shocked when she put it on. What was wrong? It had been made with care and love. There were no flaws in the material, nor errors in the way it was made. It was right in fit and length. "You see," she wrote, "What I am and what I think I am are not the same thing. The dress would have been stunning on a tall, swarthy brunette, lean and lanky, long-legged and long-necked, but it wasn't for a short, pudgy, graying blonde. So there it hangs in my closet, a lovely, complete ensemble—a constant reminder to me that I am what I am, and not what I think I am or would like to be."

Be honest with yourself before God. Don't try to pattern after someone else.

Come to Jesus Christ, the only source of truth. He said, ". . . I am the way, and the truth and the life; no one comes to the Father, but by me" (John 14:6). He has the ability to counteract your own inability to be totally honest with yourself and with him. He has the ability to counteract your inability to live the kind of life you'd like to live. His blood was shed for your imperfections. He died for your sins. Jesus Christ calls you to confession. Admit what is blocking your relationship with him. He knows it already. Be honest with him. Let him know in your own words the difficult time you're having accepting him as Savior. Or, perhaps, you have to admit to him what a difficult time you're having accepting him as Lord.

Dishonesty with God is naïveté. Naïveté like that of the hurricane party crowd at the Richelieu Apartments in Pass Christian, Mississippi. These young married couples were happy, gay, laughing, completely ignoring the hurricane moving up through the Gulf. Remember the hurricane named Camille? Chief of Police Jerry Peralta made four trips to their merry hurricane celebration. He begged and pleaded with them to leave. They laughed at him. The next morning thirteen of them were among the twenty dead found in the building's wreckage. Sure, you can pretend that you can handle your own life. You can pretend to hide your sin from God. Granted, faith is risky business because it demands our entire life. But all the odds are on God's side. He offers us forgiveness, redemption, new life in Christ.

You may be playing a risky game. Perhaps you're in inward rebellion against God. You're not willing to receive Jesus Christ. Your ego is too big. You're caught up in alcohol. You're caught up in adultery. You're taking advantage of your partner. You're overbearing on your kids. Your business is your god. Pick your commandment. You've broken it. You know what your hang-up is that is blocking your contact with God. Get honest about it. Quit bearing false witness to yourself before him. Get down on your knees in honesty with yourself and claim his forgiveness, his love, his spiritual power which you need.

Look yourself in the eye. Hold up the mirror of God's Word, which may reflect some things you don't want to see. But look deeply into that mirror and you will see the image of the Risen Christ whose outstretched, nail-pierced hands beckon to you. His loving, gracious voice says, "Be honest with others, yourself, and me. Come unto me with all your good, bad, and indifferent and I will set you free!"

"You shall not covet your neighbor's house; you shall not covet your neighbor's wife, or his manservant, or his maidservant, or his ox, or his ass, or anything that is your neighbor's."

*Exodus 20:17*

# 11.
# CURING THE CANCER
# OF DISCONTENT

AT AGE 26 she had everything a girl could want. At least it seemed that way. She attended Catalina School for Girls, had a sumptuous debut and graduated from Radcliffe as a bright, well-educated young woman. She traveled in Europe. She worked in a museum in San Francisco, then at a bookstore in New York. She campaigned for Robert Kennedy and took care of children in Watts. She was heiress of a coffee fortune, able to afford anything she wanted. She wanted more! Covetous of a relationship with a boyfriend, she plunged deeper and deeper into an aimless quest for contentment. It led her into the weird world of narcotics usage until it all ended abruptly one August night at an isolated hilltop home in Bel Air, California. She was one of the Charles Manson victims. Her name? Abigail Folger.

He had everything a man could want. He had worked his way from a modest beginning in agriculture to a place of prominence in his country's army. He was a man destined to great things. Being a war hero was not all. He moved into politics. By popular acclaim, he became his nation's chief executive. He was married. He had vast financial resources. He claimed to be a man of God. Seething within him was a spirit of covetousness, an inner discontent, which caused him to eye another woman. She was the wife of one of his friends. His covetousness led to adultery. The adultery led to murder. His name? David. God's anointed. The King of Israel.

Covetousness is a sign of discontent. It's the inner restless yearning for something that is not one's own. It's revealed in the frenzied quest for happiness of Abigail Folger and the lack of satisfaction which marked King David. Exodus 20:17 concludes the Ten Commandments, saying: "You shall not covet your neighbor's house; you shall not covet your neighbor's wife, or his manservant, or his maidservant, or his ox, or his ass, or anything that is your neighbor's."

Obviously this is not a human commandment. There's no way it could be. Why not? Because there's no way that human beings could police this tendency. You can make a person take a day off. You can penalize the murderer. You can ostracize the adulterer. You can prosecute the thief. You can pretty quickly identify the liar. But covetousness goes beneath public conduct. It touches at the motivational level, which society cannot patrol. It takes God to probe deeply into our inner motivations in a way that roots out those attitudes which can produce outward antisocial behavior.

This Tenth Commandment is God's way of stating a final "don't" which sets us free—for he calls us to be satisfied with what we have. The person who covets his neighbor's house is not satisfied with God's protection from the elements. The person who lusts after the marriage partner of another is expressing his discontent with the spouse God has given to him. The individual who stands in envy of the things which belong to another is a man waving his fist in God's face, demanding more of him than he may see fit to give. Isn't covetousness really an inner insatiable desire to live at the world's standard, not at God's? When I covet, don't I doubt God's goodness? Am I not questioning his wisdom? Isn't it my tendency to feel under-privileged? Isn't it my orientation to let my wants drive me? Isn't covetousness my endeavor to judge my success or failure on the basis of what others have, constantly comparing myself to another? Isn't it the way in which I label myself rich or poor, not by how much I consume, but what I think I should con-sume? In the process I'm driven on, wanting more of what others have that I think I don't have.

For some of us, covetousness is simply a desire for good things which has gone out of control. For others of us, it is a desire for those things which are unlawful, or our endeavor to pursue lawful things in an unlawful way. For all of us, covetousness is the subtle determination that we need more than we really do.

I find this the most difficult of the Ten Commandments. Up to this point, I'm right with God. That doesn't mean I haven't broken, either in action or attitude, each of the others. I have. I don't really have a problem with them in that I know how right they are and I want to live by them. But this one I don't find so easy. There's something about me which makes con-stant comparisons with others. I know no other way to measure myself. And then I get to thinking, what is there within me which makes me want to measure myself in comparison to others? Am I really that insecure? Am I really that uncertain that God has created me as someone special? So instead I chase after other people. I want their prestige, their attractiveness, their good looks, their intelligence, their athletic ability, their manners to rub off on me. And you know—enough never quite rubs off, so I want more.

Then I read the Bible. It says that God created me to live in this world but not to live in bondage to it. Things are important. The Bible says much about life's necessities. Then God tells me that I am not to be in bondage to things. I'm not to live a worldly existence in which things monopolize me. I'm to live in a spiritual dimension of fellowship with God in which the things he's given are used for the productive end of glorifying God and enjoying him forever.

What is it that covetousness does to a person? Why is it that God would devote so much of his Word to fingering this tendency which each of us has?

One reason is that covetousness kills our contentment. As long as we look at other people and see what they have and judge our own satisfaction in comparison to what they possess, we'll be discontented. We'll never experience full satisfaction. We'll keep grabbing and grabbing. The more we have the less happy we'll be. If we're not successful at grabbing, we'll be all the more discontent with our modest circumstances. Proverbs 23:4–5 recommends: "Do not toil to acquire wealth; be wise enough to desist. When your eyes light upon it, it is gone; for suddenly it takes to itself wings, flying like an eagle toward heaven."

You'll never get what you want. The wants get bigger and bigger and often your very possessions become your captor.

No one ever learned this a harder way than the man who wrote Ecclesiastes. He had already been "jilted" by wine, women, song, and power. He knew what he was talking about when he said: "He who loves money will not be satisfied with money; nor he who loves wealth, with gain; this also is vanity. When goods increase, they increase who eat them; and what gain has their owner but to see them with his eyes?" (Eccles. 5:10–11).

The Bible speaks in favor of good hard work. The Bible endorses the right to own private property. In fact, many verses give tribute to the person who has been industrious. In some cases material wealth is a sign of God's blessing. It's not that wealth is wrong; it's the compulsive desire to have more and more that destroys people. It takes away satisfaction and kills contentment. It's that grasping attitude which seems to believe that it is more blessed to receive than to give. This kind of person pulls all his possessions in around him so tightly, determined to hold onto everything and grab even more.

D. L. Moody used to tell the story about a millionaire in France. In order to make sure of his wealth, this miser dug a cave in his wine cellar so large and so deep that he would go down into it with a ladder. The entrance had a door with a spring lock. After a time, he was missing. A search revealed no trace of him. At last his house was sold and the purchaser discovered the door in the cellar. He opened it, went down, and found the miser lying dead on the ground in the midst of his riches. The door must have shut accidentally after him. He perished miserably.

This selfish, acquisitive spirit of covetousness guarantees that we'll never get what we want and kills our contentment in the process.

Another reason God warns so much about covetousness is that it has a way of monopolizing life. It will con us, leading us away from what we were meant to be. Strangely enough, those of us who are called to full-time gospel ministry are particularly susceptible. Paul urged young Timothy both to be personally on guard and to warn his church members that Satan can lead a person far away from the Lord by stimulating within him a covetous spirit. Paul wrote:

There is great gain in godliness with contentment; for we brought nothing into the world, and we cannot take anything out of the world; but if we have food and clothing, with these we shall be content. But those who desire to be rich fall into temptation, into a snare, into many senseless and hurtful desires that plunge men into ruin and destruction. For the love of money is the root of all evils; it is through this craving that some have wandered away from the faith and pierced their hearts with many pangs (1 Tim. 6:6–10).

The Bible is studded with such examples. Lot tricked his generous uncle, Abraham, out of the best land. He loved the fancy life of Sodom. Years later he had to escape for his life. All his equity was left behind. Think of those wasted years.

Then there was Balaam. He's referred to as a false prophet. Actually, all his prophecies turned out to be correct. He was faithful to the Word, but Satan finally nailed him with covetousness. He sold his soul to God's enemies.

You know Gehazi. He was Elisha's righthand man. He just couldn't resist profiteering. He ended up with some temporary possessions, but he also picked up Naaman's leprosy. He lost the friendship of Elisha. (How many of us today, driven by our quest for material things, destroy our health and lose the friendship of our loved ones?)

We've already mentioned David. There's no question that Bathsheba, Uriah's wife, was "very beautiful to look upon." There are many attractive women in the world. Entertain the thoughts that say, "I want what I'm not entitled to," long enough and you'll be driven wild with frustrated passion. Or you'll relieve that inner tension by acting out what produces adultery and even murder.

You see, there's no relationship between how much you have and how much more you want. When Nathan told about a man who had many sheep, but coveted the single lamb of the poor man, David had no question. Any man who owned all those sheep and was so possessive of them that he was ready to steal the only sheep owned by another—that man deserved to die. David couldn't see that he was that man. He had a moral perspective when it came to others. His own acquisitiveness had monopolized his sensitivities.

Then there's another reason to avoid covetousness. Not only does it kill contentment and monopolize energies, it also shrinks the soul and destroys one's taste for what is best. One of the most haunting phrases in the Bible comes as the Psalmist describes the fickle attitude of the Israelites. They had their ups and downs. They were tough on Moses. And they made their demands on God. The King James Version says that they lusted exceedingly in the wilderness and tempted God in the desert, "and he gave them their request but sent leanness into their soul" (Ps. 106:15). Sometimes God will give you and me what we want. It may not be what's best. We grab and grab and get what we want. In the process we become spiritually impoverished, discontent with what God has given, grasping for more and more. We are unwilling to share our tithes and offerings. Keeping careful accounts of what is mine and what is yours can disqualify us from inheriting the Kingdom of God. Look at the company into which God places the covetous, greedy person.

> Do you not know that the unrighteous will not inherit the kingdom of God? Do not be deceived; neither the immoral, nor idolaters, nor adulterers, nor sexual perverts, nor thieves, nor the greedy, nor drunkards, nor revilers, nor robbers will inherit the kingdom of God. And such were some of you. But you were washed, you were sanctified, you were justified in the name of the Lord Jesus Christ and in the Spirit of our God (1 Cor. 6: 9–11).

How I wish I could get away from having to confront the truth of this command. It demands of me much spiritual introspection. It insists that I take a look at the world in which I live and increasingly make lifestyle decisions thoughtful of others, more freely investing in the spiritual and physical needs of this world which our Lord has entrusted to us.

Remember the farmer Jesus told about? He became more and more successful. He took pride in what he had accomplished. He determined to tear down his barns and build larger ones so he could store all his grain. And then he paused to remind himself that he had taken care of his security in this life. Now he could take it easy—eating, drinking, and making merry. At that precise moment God said to him "Fool! This night your soul is required of you; and the things you have prepared, whose will they be?"

Why is it that Jesus calls this man a fool? It's interesting to note that Jesus does not rebuke this man for his affluence. What he does do is chide him for two attitudes. One is that he thought only of himself. The other is that he had failed to make provision for the future life. This man had been so caught up in things here and now, laying up treasures for himself on earth, that he was spiritually poverty-stricken. In fact Jesus uses these striking opening words, ". . . Take heed, and beware of all covetousness; for a man's life does not consist in the abundance of his possessions" (Luke 12:15).

With God's help, I'm going to listen to this Tenth Commandment. With God's help, I'm not going to let the good things of this world make a fool of me by letting them capture my soul. With God's help, I'm going to ride loose in the saddle, putting the tithe right up front where it belongs, giving additional gifts to the Lord, and trying somehow to invest my life more faithfully in his service.

The same thing may happen to you or me that happened to Bishop Festo Kivengere. In a matter of hours he lost everything. He'd worked hard to build a home. He had material possessions. When "push" came to "shove" and President Amin demanded that the Christians subordinate their Christian values to his values, Bishop Kivengere was willing to give up every material possession instead of compromising his faith. I hope I've got that moral and spiritual resiliency. It sure would be easy to rationalize. God help me to ride more loosely in the saddle.

Periodically we need to check ourselves out to see whether or not we've become covetous to the point of living in bondage to the things of this world. I've jotted down several questions. Perhaps they can serve as a checklist alerting us as to whether our lives are being dictated by a lusting after things or are being lived in harmony with spiritual values.

Question One: Where are my thoughts? Are they wholly worldly? A Christian's thoughts are primarily geared toward the Kingdom of God. They're thoughts of those who live in anticipation of spending eternity with Jesus Christ. The covetous person's thoughts are primarily in this world constantly plotting for some kind of personal gain.

Question Two: Am I exerting more energy in getting the things of this world than I'm exerting in an endeavor to attain the things of heaven? Where is my effort being put? Laying up treasures where moth and rust corrupt? Or am I busy in service for your Savior Jesus Christ in a way which enables others to spend eternity with him?

Question Three: What topics monopolize my conversation? Are they always people, things, and the ideas of this world? Or is there some inner urgency in conversation about the things of God which are of this world but go beyond it?

Question Four: Is my heart so set on the things of this world that my relationship to Jesus Christ will be parted with for a price? In other words, how important is my business success? My social standing? My high school athletic career? My dating life? Are these the highest goals for me to the point that if backed to a wall, Jesus Christ would come off on the short end of the deal?

Question Five: Do I have so many irons in the fire that I have no time for God? Do I have lame excuses as to why I cannot serve Christ in the study of Scripture? In prayer? In the sharing of my faith? In church attendance? In places of responsible Christian service?

Question Six: Will I obtain my ends in this world by any means, even if these involve wrongdoing of some kind? Am I so devoted to a master other than Jesus Christ that I will distort what I know is right in the service of that other master?

Where do you stand in terms of these questions? Do any of them alert you that perhaps your priorities have become distorted to the point that you are basically discontent with what God has given to you? This command of God's isn't for a moment calling us to a life void of satisfaction. It's not calling us to repudiate material possessions. It's calling us to a life with a fullness of meaning and purpose that otherwise is impossible when we allow ourselves to be caught up with a craving for things good in themselves, but distorting to our relationship with Jesus Christ.

Actually, those of us who are discontent have failed to take God at his word. One of two things is wrong: we are basically divided into one or another of two categories.

One category of discontented people is made up of those who have failed to take God at his word in terms of his promise of salvation. He created us for a purpose. He states clearly that every single person has rebelled against him. We've all tried to run our own lives. There's not a person who can deny that ego and self is so often the motivating factor. God continues to say that his love is a constant love. It caused him to become a man. To live as we live. To experience the problems we experience. To die the criminal's death on the crude cross bearing our sins and our rebellion and rising from the dead literally, bodily triumphant over sin. The facts are there. They can be questioned. Nonetheless they stand etched in human history claiming to be God's provision to meet the human discontent which comes as the result of sin.

God invites us to receive Jesus Christ as our Savior. He urges us to express our sorrow, to repent. He urges us to turn around and walk away from our sin. He senses our discontent.

Perhaps you've been hanging around church all your life because you want the fringe benefits of Christianity. Now the time has come for decision. You are discontent with life the way it is. Yet you've not received the assurance of salvation because you're holding back on giving yourself to Christ. Your worldly concerns continue to attract you. You've not come to the point that you're willing to say, "I'm sorry I have distorted values. I'm seeking the wrong goals. I'm willing now to give myself 100 percent to Jesus Christ in faith claiming Christ's promise of salvation." God promises eternal life right now. And he promises to release you from hell in the life to come; that you may spend eternity with him in heaven.

There's a second category of discontented people. It's made up of Christians who are failing to take God at his word. You may fall into this category. You have received Jesus Christ as Savior. You've had an experience with Jesus at some time in the past. Now the fresh bloom of that love is no longer there. You've leveled off in your devotions. You no longer have the craving desire to share Christ with others as you once did. You're no longer living in the reality of his promise that he will supply your every need according to his riches in glory by Christ Jesus. Therefore you're becoming preoccupied with things. You take care of yourself and your family. Business is emerging as primary. Your social life has become more important than it once was. Whereas there was a day when you served Christ faithfully in his church, looking forward to fellowship with other Christians, you now almost dread these exercises because they only alert you to what once was and no longer is.

This can happen so easily. You can reach out trying to blame someone else for what has taken place. Or you can become inverted into an internalized questioning as to whether your original relationship with Jesus was anything more than some emotional experience which would last only temporarily. In the meantime, you stand juggling the things of God and the things of man as far as your affections are concerned. You know that the things of God are better, but you find the things of man more momentarily attractive. Your problem is you're not taking God at his word. You're not living in present tense, vital, everyday faith. You're caught up in the past tense, trying to recapture what happened before, not believing that God is sufficient to provide your every need in the present.

The Apostle Paul went through many ups and downs in his outward circumstances. In a highly personal way, he often shared both his good times and his bad times in his biblical writings. He related how he had learned "in whatever state I am, to be content." Claiming that he knew how to be abased and how to abound, how to be full and how to be hungry, he went on to say, "I can do all things in him who strengthens me" (Phil. 4:11–13). The vital Christian life is a life lived in the present. Look to the past only for the confirmation that God has been present. Live in His presence now. This is a life that goes with Christ even when times get difficult and the prosperity of those who do not know Christ looks awfully good. It's a life that remains faithful to the Lord when times go good, when your affluence is great. It's a life which seeks first the Kingdom of God and His righteousness and then discovers God's blessings.

Abigail Folger had it all but was discontent. She coveted after a peace of mind which she never received in her frenetically aimless quest. It was available to her and it is to you, the non-Christian who's looking for something. Give yourself to Christ. Trust him to cure your cancer of discontent.

King David, the man of God, got off on a sidetrack for a while. In his discontent, he sinned. How gracious is our God. In Psalm 51 we see the spiritually backslidden David get down on his knees and cry for the mercy of God to enable him to once again live with the presence of God's spirit. In repentance he called out for cleansing. He claimed a clean heart, a right spirit. From the depths of his heart, he cried out to God the prayer that should be on the lips of every Christian who yearns for a curing of the cancer of discontent, "Restore unto me the joy of thy salvation."

> "Think not that I have come to abolish the law and the prophets; I have come not to abolish them but to fulfil them."
>
> *Matthew 5:17*

# 12.
# THE ALL-FULFILLING CHRIST

WE'VE SPENT a lot of time talking about the Ten Commandments. Perhaps by now you're raising some questions. Why so much talk about the law? Aren't we living in an age of grace?

Yes. But God's ushering in grace does not destroy the law. Jesus did not come to shatter the Old Testament traditions. Here's what he said about himself:

"Think not that I have come to abolish the law and the prophets; I have come not to abolish them but to fulfill them. For truly, I say to you, till heaven and earth pass away, not an iota, not a dot, will pass from the law until all is accomplished. Whoever then relaxes one of the least of these commandments and teaches men so, shall be called least in the kingdom of heaven; but he who does them and teaches them shall be called great in the kingdom of heaven. For I tell you, unless your righteousness exceeds that of the scribes and Pharisees, you will never enter the kingdom of heaven" (Matt. 5:17–20).

Far from being the abolisher of the law, Jesus is the fulfiller of the law. All of our emphasis on grace is poorly based if we think that God's law does not apply to today. It does. When Jesus said that he came not to abolish the law and the prophets but to fulfill them, he meant precisely what he said. Jesus kept the moral law. He was obedient to the Ten Commandments.

Not only that. We've already seen how Jesus is the all-fulfilling Christ because he filled those moral teachings with a deeper understanding that they'd ever had before. He took the commandment against murder and broadened it to anyone who angrily insulted his brother. He expanded the teaching against the practice of adultery to include the lustful thought. Far from abolishing it, he deepened it. He gave to it that enlarged meaning which it was intended to hold.

However, if you try to save yourself and win a right relationship with God by obeying his law, you are in trouble. The law is good. You are to obey it. Salvation by grace does not do away with God's law in the principles that it articulates. It continues to function in the three ways we've already mentioned—none of which bring salvation.

The first function of the law is to serve as a "policeman" in a society made up of unregenerate men and women. The law of God clearly establishes principles on which society must be built if there is to be freedom for human beings to exist with any kind of personal fulfillment. Murder, adultery, dishonesty, and all of the other matters spoken to by the law will, if they are not held in check, bring back the dissolution of that culture.

The second function of the law is the way in which it serves as a "convictor," alerting unsaved men and women to their basic sinfulness. It is only when we see what God would have us be that we're truly aware of our failure. It is only in the light of our human need that we are drawn to him in repentance, seeking his forgiveness.

The third use of the law is that of "schoolmaster," in which you and I respond to God's grace in a way that makes us want to do his will. We are aware that his grace is what saves us. It's not our works. It's our love for him that makes us yearn to do his will. We are instructed by the law. We never depend upon our obedience for salvation. We do genuinely desire to do that which will please our Lord.

But let's underline this fact once and for all. As good as God's law is in policing society, convicting of sin, and serving as a schoolmaster for believers—God's law has never saved anyone. Why? Because nobody has ever completely obeyed it. That's where Jesus Christ steps into the scene.

Jesus is the all-fulfilling Christ. Why is this? He fulfills the law not only by elaborating on its principles; he gives to it the added dimension of love.

Jesus taught a fundamental, ethical principle. It was that evil cannot be destroyed by evil. Evil can only be destroyed by love.

Remember that day when the Pharisees tried to trick Jesus, asking him which was the great commandment in the law. He said to them:

"... You shall love the Lord your God with all your heart, and with all your soul, and with all your mind. This is the great and first commandment. And a second is like it. You shall love your neighbor as yourself. On these two commandments depend all the law and the prophets" (Matt. 22:37–40).

This is a revolutionary concept. First, Jesus takes the Old Testament law and applies it to our thought life, to our attitudes. Now he elaborates on it, undergirding it with a much deeper principle called love. There's a difference between law and legalism. You know people who are pedantically precise. They do everything right. They pride themselves in following

Emily Post or Amy Vanderbilt to the letter. They're aggravating persons in their perfectionistic bent. They have their etiquette down cold. Some such persons have the technicality of the law but not the spirit. The very etiquette which should reflect good manners is repulsive. They are sterile legalists.

For example, the Old Testament law allowed "an eye for an eye and a tooth for a tooth" in the case of personal injury. Jesus said, "Don't return evil for evil. If anyone strikes you on the right cheek, turn him the other also." Jesus said, "If anyone would sue you and take your coat, let him have your cloak as well. If an official forces you to go one mile, voluntarily go two. If someone begs from you, don't refuse him. Don't turn him away."

These are explosive teachings. Some would say that Jesus taught pacifism. I question this. However, not even a pacifist stands by when a helpless woman or child is attacked. What Jesus means is that at no point are you and I to give way to revenge. A Christian's attitude is not to be one of retaliation. We are to allow the spirit of God to overcome our hatred with love. We're to go so far as to love our enemies and pray for those who persecute us.

But this is not all. Jesus is not the all-fulfilling Christ just because he deepens our understanding of the Old Testament law or because he introduces the principle of love in its highest intellectual ideal. He's not the all-fulfilling Christ just because he was the greatest ethical teacher who modeled the ultimate in love. No, there's even a much greater way in which he is the all-fulfilling Christ. When Jesus said that he had come not to abolish the law and the prophets but to fulfill them. He is also making reference to the ceremonial law and the prophetic utterances of the prophets. This is why John the Baptist cried out, ". . . Behold, the Lamb of God, who takes away the sin of the world!" (John 1:29). Jesus not only models the ultimate in love; he is ultimate love. He is God become man. He carried out the two most cataclysmic acts in all human history.

First, he died for the human race. That's why he came to earth. He came to die. That's what Isaiah was talking about when he prophesied:

> Surely he has born our griefs and carried our sorrows; yet we esteemed him stricken, smitten by God, and afflicted. But he was wounded for our transgressions, he was bruised for our iniquities; upon him was the chastisement that made us whole, and with his stripes we are healed (Isa. 53:4–5).

Do you see the picture? This Jesus is the fulfillment of all the law and the prophets. He is the One, and the only One, who could set the human race straight after the fall of Adam and Eve. He's the only One who could bruise the head of the serpent. He's the only One who could take the place of the innocent lamb symbolically slain by the priests in the temple. The angel of death passed over when it saw the blood smeared above the door during the Exodus. Satan's power over you is destroyed when he sees the shed blood of Jesus Christ poured out on the cross as an atonement for your sin.

Yes, that's what he came for—to die. He came to die for your failure to keep the law. You just can't do it. Neither can I. That implies that you and I are both helpless, doesn't it? I don't like that any better than you. It's absolutely correct! The law in all of its good functions cannot save. That's why we need a Savior. Jesus Christ fulfills the law. He does it by filling the gap between the ideal, that pristine keeping of both the Old Testament legal codes and the New Testament law of love, and the reality of our existence. He is the embodiment of love as he is nailed to the cross. There he is bearing the tremendous weight of your sin and mine.

My heart cries out in awe at this glorious thought. Not only did this all-fulfilling Christ die for the human race. Second, he rose from the dead in victory over sin and death.

This is the Easter message: the grave could not contain him. His was no ordinary crucifixion. Men had died on crosses before; men would die on crosses again. Many good men and women have died martyrs for their faith. We call them saints. But Jesus is not a saint. This One who died on the cross bearing the sins of the world is now the Risen Lord. The literal resurrection of Jesus Christ from the dead is the greatest event in all human history.

Some debunk it. They say it never happened. Even some modern so-called Christian theologians play verbal games referring to "the resurrection event." They make it hazy. Perhaps it happened. Perhaps not. They say it doesn't make any difference. It's what happens to individual lives who experience this somewhat foggy, philosophical resurrection principle.

The New Testament unequivocally states that Jesus Christ bodily rose from the dead. The Apostle Luke talks about "many infallible proofs." Some would deny this simply because they don't believe in miracles. They can't accept the fact that someone could rise from the dead. What they're really saying is they can't believe that there's such a thing as a God who has supernatural power. If there is a God who is all-powerful, he certainly has the ability to resurrect his crucified Son.

Some would laugh at Luke's infallible proofs. They would say these so-called proofs are based on witnesses who could have been having hallucinations. If you want to play that game, you could question the existence of George Washington. All history is based on witnesses. There's the fact of the empty tomb.

It stands in the way of all attempts to explain away the resurrection. Why didn't the authorities produce the body? It was to their benefit to crush a nonfactual rumor. There were the precisely disposed grave clothes. There are the numerous appearances over nearly six weeks. He appeared to Mary Magdalene. He met the two disciples on the Emmaus road. He confronted the disciples in the locked room when Thomas was present. He appeared to the seven at the Sea of Galilee. He appeared to the five hundred. He appeared to James. The very existence of the Christian church bears witness to the fact that something happened to transform a broken, beaten group of losers into men and women who gave their very lives for the Christ whom they had witnessed in his resurrection power. Sunday is the Lord's Day. We worship on the first day of the week, not the seventh. The first day is the day of resurrection.

Jesus in his post-ascension power revealed himself to the Apostle John. He said, ". . . Fear not, I am the first and the last, and the living one; I died, and behold I am alive for evermore, and I have the keys of Death and Hades" (Rev. 1:17–18). Jesus said to his friends at Bethany when he raised his close friend Lazarus from the dead, ". . . I am the resurrection and the life; he who believes in me, though he die, yet shall he live, and whoever lives and believes in me shall never die . . ." (John 11:25–26).

The Apostle Paul hit the issue head-on with the church at Corinth. There were skeptics who denied the resurrection of the body then as there are now. Paul was quick to say that if it didn't happen, those of us who call ourselves Christians are to be pitied. He put it in these words:

Now if Christ is preached as raised from the dead, how can some of you say that there is no resurrection of the dead? But if there is no resurrection of the dead, then Christ has not been raised, then our preaching is in vain and your faith is in vain. We are even found to be misrepresenting God, because we testified of God that he raised Christ, whom he did not raise if it is true that the dead are not raised. For if the dead are not raised, then Christ has not been raised. If Christ has not been raised, your faith is futile and you are still in your sins. Then those also who have fallen asleep in Christ have perished. If for this life only we have hoped in Christ, we are of all men most to be pitied (1 Cor. 15:12–19).

Jesus is the all-fulfilling Christ because through his death and resurrection he releases you from the bondage of the law. You are no longer lost because of your inability to obey the law's letter. If you have repented of your sins and trusted him, he forgives everything.

Yes, his is total forgiveness. Every sin which has marked your life is totally forgiven. Perhaps you're going through life bogged down with guilt. You know you've done wrong. Sin is clearly defined by him. But now grace reigns. You are totally forgiven. You are just as if you had never sinned. Do you believe this? Stop a moment. Think about it. Do you really believe it? If so, why then do you allow yourself that tortured memory? God says that through Christ he has removed your transgressions as far as the east is from the west. No, God doesn't wink at sin. He doesn't take it lightly. He's not asking you to develop a casual attitude toward sin. Your active or passive rebellion against God demanded the greatest act of love in human history. Your sin and mine nailed Jesus to the tree. Let me assure you on the authority of God's Word, that sacrifice was efficacious. It was complete. You can have a clean slate before God, before your fellowmen, and before yourself, if you will genuinely confess your sins and ask his forgiveness.

But, no, you're determined to hold on to it. You won't let

go, will you? You won't take him at his word. Your sin is too great for him, isn't it? The only sin that is too great for him to forgive is your refusal to accept his forgiveness. Let him clean you up. I urge you. I urge you as "one beggar showing another beggar where to get bread."

Jesus is the all-fulfilling Christ because through his death and resurrection he removes the sting from death. In our fast-moving technological era, death is right around the corner for all of us. Jesus doesn't keep us from dying. Through his death and resurrection, he does keep us from staying dead. The Bible describes a mystery. You and I will not stay asleep. We shall all be changed in a moment, in the twinkling of an eye. The dead will be raised imperishable. You and I will be changed. This perishable nature will put on the imperishable. Our mortal bodies will become immortal. Death is swallowed up in victory. Where is death's victory? Where is death's sting? "The sting of death is sin, and the power of sin is the law. But thanks be to God, who gives us the victory through our Lord Jesus Christ" (1 Cor. 15:56–57).

Jesus has taken the sting out of death. The sting is sin.

How exciting it is to observe the hope which marks the life of a true believer in Jesus Christ. I'll never forget my conversation with Joe Bayly. He's written a book titled *The View from a Hearse*. He's certainly qualified. Joe has lost three sons of his own to death. We talked at length about some of the latest studies in the area of death and dying. Then Joe's face brightened as he shared his confidence that there's a light at the end of the long, dark tunnel called death—the light of eternity in the presence of Jesus Christ.

Jesus is the all-fulfilling Christ because through his death and resurrection, he promises us eternal God-life right here and now. Jesus is the embodiment of life. Eternal life is not just that which goes on and on. Frankly, I wouldn't be too interested in everlasting life if it meant the continuing day-in and day-out existence that I experience when I'm not in right relationship with God. Eternal life is that quality living which he enables right now.

Jesus Christ can transform your present living to be what it was meant to be. He's in the business of remaking persons. He does it every day. No, he won't take away your problems. Instead, he'll give you the strength to face them. Jesus is an enabler who will recreate you by his Spirit into his image. We're hearing a lot of talk about being "born again." That's what it's all about. It's a process of spiritual regeneration. It involves your being willing to say yes to God, not only in allowing Jesus Christ to come into your life as Savior, but it involves allowing him to be Lord of your existence.

This is eternal life. It's a whole lifestyle in which you're free both to die and to live. Christ can strip from you the uptightness, the fear, the anxiety which may very well mark your existence.

Several years ago I was driven in a pick-up truck from a mission station in Addis Ababa, Ethiopia out to the International Airport. The driver was Donald McClure, a seventy-year-old retired Presbyterian missionary. Seldom have I seen a man so filled with enthusiasm for life. After clearing security, we drove on to the airport apron. Joined by several others, we loaded a DC-3 cargo plane with irrigation supplies for a mission station in Omo. Retired in name only, Don McClure gave his every effort to the loading process right alongside the rest of us much younger men. He handled our international airline tickets while we flew to the mission outposts. His wife took in our laundry. A few days later, we returned to Addis Ababa. Don was there with the revalidated tickets and the carefully folded laundry. The next morning he picked us up at 6:30 and drove us to the airport to catch our flight back to the States. He gave me a silver Ethiopian cross for Anne whom he had never met. And he handed me a woven Ethiopian cross.

A few days later, my friend Don McClure was shot at by a group of bandits and killed at the Godi Mission Station on the Somalia-Ethiopia border.

No, don't shed any tears for Don McClure. He knew how to live. And he knew how to die. The tears are for those of us who remain. Or better stated, the tears are for those of us who never met the all-fulfilling Christ whose death and resurrection release us from the bondage of the law, remove the sting of death, and equip us to have eternal life right here and now.

# NOTES

## Chapter 2
1. Maclaren, Alexander, *Expositions of Holy Scripture*, "Exodus, Leviticus, and Numbers" (Cincinnati: Jennings and Graham; New York: Eaton and Mains), pp. 97–98.

## Chapter 3
1. Joy Davidman, *Smoke on the Mountain* (Philadelphia: Westminster Press, 1970).

## Chapter 4
1. Thomas Watson, *The Ten Commandments* (London: The Banner of Truth Trust; first published as part of *A Body of Practical Divinity*, 1692; revised reprint, 1965).

## Chapter 5
1. Arthur Fay Sueltz, *New Directions from the Ten Commandments* (New York: Harper & Row, 1976), p. 39.
2. November 5, 1972.

## Chapter 6
1. Quoted in John Vander Ploeg, "I Taught Him to Obey," *The Presbyterian Journal*, May 7, 1969, p. 8.

## Chapter 7
1. Sueltz, *New Directions from the Ten Commandments*, p. 59.
2. Quoted by Dr. Joel Nederhood, "Thinking About Abortion,"

*The Back to God Hour* radio program of the Christian Reformed Church.

Chapter 8

1. Albert Rosenfeld, "Science, Sex and Tomorrow's Morality," *Life*, June, 1969.
2. C. S. Lewis, *Mere Christianity* (New York: Macmillan, 1960), p. 92.
3. December 8, 1976, p. 1097.
4. *Miami Herald*, 1977.

Chapter 9

1. Sueltz, *New Directions from the Ten Commandments*, pp. 82–83.
2. New York: Simon and Schuster, 1977.

Chapter 10

1. T. Robert Ingram, *The World under God's Law* (Houston, TX: St. Thomas Press, 1970).
2. *The Presbyterian Journal*, May 7, 1969, p. 11.